D0197840

China
Call

Leonard Bolton

Gospel Publishing House
Springfield, Missouri

02-0509

Library of Congress Catalog Card Number 83-82031
International Standard Book Number 0-88243-509-4
Printed in the United States of America

To Ada
A Sweet Wife and Mother
who held lightly to things,
but tenaciously to the Lord!

Her children arise up, and call her blessed;
her husband also, and he praiseth her.
Proverbs 31:28

Contents

Foreword

Catching world attention today is a mighty move of the Holy Spirit in the country of Burma. Hundreds of indigenous, vibrant churches are helping to shape the destiny of a nation. As a field, Burma is considered one of the most outstanding examples of missionary work in the history of missions.

The question naturally follows, How did this great work begin? Where did it begin? The answer can be found quite easily. The Pentecostal testimony was brought to Burma by one of the greatest pioneer missionaries—Leonard Bolton. He, followed by such stalwart missionaries as Clifford and Lavada Morrison, planted the seed so well, laid down such correct principles of missions strategy, that the seed was bound to bring forth a mighty harvest.

Many stirring books have been written about the lives and ministries of missionaries. But some stories have not been told. This book represents one of these untold stories.

Missionary pioneers Leonard and Ada Bolton, along with the Lewers and others, made their way through incredible difficulties— by river boat and dugout, on horseback, on foot, in sedan chair, on the backs of coolies—to the remote area of the Far East where Tibet, China, and Burma meet. Oblivious to hardship and overwhelmed with a passion for souls, the Boltons saw a revival there among the primitive tribal people: the Lisu, Nung, Rawang, Kanong, and Maru. Today this whole area is Christianized; it has seen a mighty move of Pentecostal power.

As you read this book, your appreciation for pioneer missionaries Leonard and Ada Bolton will grow. You will weep. You will rejoice. You are sharing one of the greatest stories of Pentecostal missionary adventure and triumph.

It has been my privilege to work with hundreds of great missionary pioneers. But not one is greater than the Boltons!

> MAYNARD KETCHAM
> FIELD DIRECTOR EMERITUS
> EAST ASIA, DIVISION OF FOREIGN MISSIONS
> THE GENERAL COUNCIL OF THE ASSEMBLIES OF GOD

Introduction

A Lisu tribesman came trudging down the mountain trail into the city of Wei-hsi, a fine fat hen tucked in the fold of his coarse hemp tunic. As he passed through the marketplace, several people observed the bird's healthy red comb and glossy feathers.

"I'll buy your chicken," offered one of them. "How much do you want for it?"

"Oh no," he replied, "I'm not selling it."

"Sell it to me," said another. "I'll give you a good price for it. Here's a silver dollar!"

"No! I'm not selling it."

"I'll give you two silver dollars!"

"No, no! I'm taking it to the Happiness News Hall to exchange it for a Book."

He turned resolutely from the temptation and walked into the mission station. A seed of gospel truth had been planted in his heart and he wanted more. He had walked for five days carrying his prize chicken. Eagerly he offered it to Ada Bolton, who in return presented him with a copy of the Lisu New Testament. Clutching the Book to his heart he jubilantly exclaimed, "Now we can have the Book in our own home!"

Others came with whatever they had to offer—perhaps only a couple of eggs or some turnips—and they received the same precious Book.

SUCH HUNGER FOR the Word of God has characterized the Lisu. Over four hundred thousand of these sturdy tribespeople live in the highlands of southwest China, upper Burma, and northern Thailand. Today, the astounding emergence of a great Pentecostal church in Burma, with more than half of its constituency Lisu, is a thrilling epoch in missions history.

To these Lisu people, God brought His messengers of truth from England, America, and Canada. At His bidding, these missionaries left family and homeland to penetrate the unknown interior of China, bringing the message of life. The Lisu received the Word gladly and held high the torch of faith through times of persecution, during World War II and later during the Communist takeover, which drove many of them into Burma where the revival continues.

Nurtured with Biblical preaching and teaching, first by missionaries and then by their own leaders, Lisu converts developed indigenous churches over widespread areas of the giant Mekong and Salween River canyons and the dense jungles of upper Burma.

The Lord confirmed His Word. Accompanying the preaching of the gospel was God's witness: signs, wonders, miracles, and gifts of the Holy Spirit (Hebrews 2:4). These supernatural features stimulated the great growth of the Lisu church.

Our story centers on two people: Leonard Bolton, from a mechanical engineer's family in England, and his wife Ada, from a Mennonite family in America's Pennsylvania-Dutch country. They poured out the best years of their lives in ministry among the Lisu of the great Mekong River region, using two languages: Mandarin Chinese and the Lisu dialect.

My wife and I have written jointly, telling this story from the perspective of Leonard Bolton, my father. As you travel my parents' road of adventure, we hope you catch some of the excitement of a missions frontier: arduous travel, primitive situations, dangerous opposition. We hope you feel a measure of the urgency to share the good news as it makes the poorest of the poor among the richest of the rich. And finally we hope you recognize the joy in obeying the call of God.

May the story of this devoted couple (and their co-workers) challenge new recruits—both in the East and in the West—to dedicate themselves fully to the Lord Jesus Christ and His Great Commission!

Primary sources for this work have been varied. They include an extensive manuscript, as well as other writings, by my sister Elsie Bolton Ezzo; letters and articles by my father and mother; and my own recollections. While preparing this book we received additional information from my mother. Photographs in China were taken and developed personally by my father.

Reference reading was from books written by Lavada Morrison, Isobel Khun, Maxine Dittemore, Dr. and Mrs. Albert Shelton, Dr. Stuart Haverson (all missionaries who served in southwest China), and Mrs. Howard Taylor, who authored J. O. Fraser's biography *Behind the Ranges.*

Articles in the *Pentecostal Evangel, The Missionary Challenge,* and *Mountain Movers* helped us to paint the Burma picture.

A word of explanation about nomenclature: Chinese names are spelled and hyphenated according to the standard Wade-Giles system of Romanization. Each syllable of a Lisu name is capitalized.

Appreciation is extended to Dr. David Woodward of the China Sunday School Union in Taiwan and to Joyce Wells Booze, writer and assistant professor of English at Central Bible College, for suggestions and encouragement.

ROBERT AND EVELYN BOLTON
TAIWAN

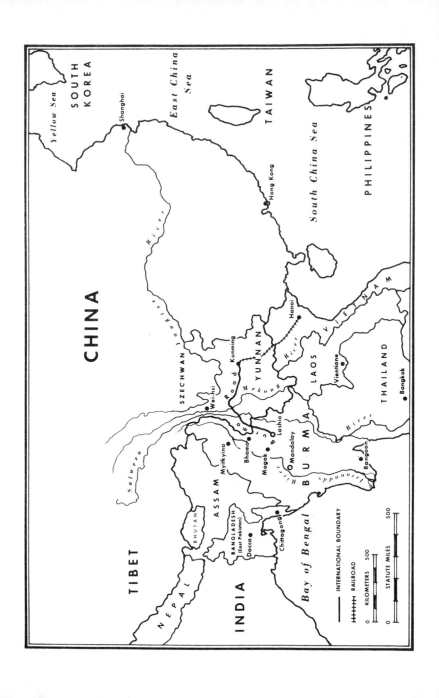

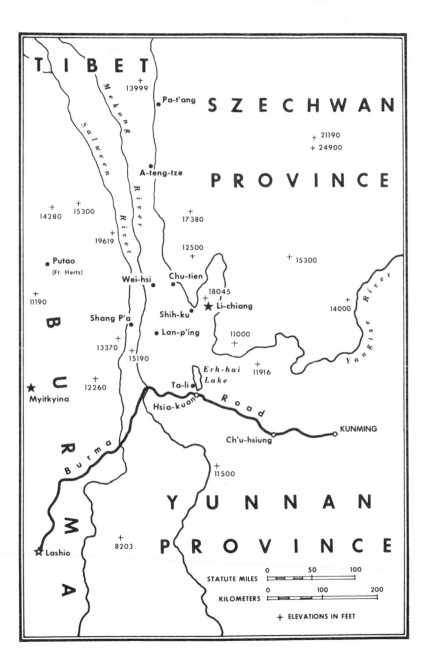

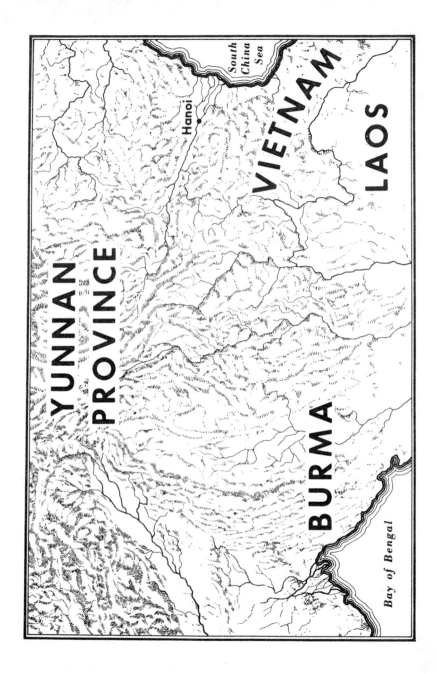

1
A Call to China

"Land!" The electrifying cry crackled throughout the ship, bringing people rushing to the deck. Olive and I ran for a glimpse of the continent on which our new venture would begin. Leaning on the railing with my arm around the small frame of my young bride, I looked into her face. The joy I saw there moved me. Our new life was not going to be easy. But she had courage and faith; she knew she was called to China.

We watched intently as indistinct forms on the horizon gradually took shape. Here and there pagodas pierced the skyline, forming a striking backdrop to the port city of Rangoon, Burma. We would be met here by Alfred Lewer. He would take us on the long journey across Burma and into the rugged mountains of southwest China to his mission station at Wei-hsi.

"Oh, Len," Olive exclaimed, "won't it be good to set foot on solid ground again and sleep on a proper bed, maybe, before starting on the trip inland! It seems like years since we left England!"

In fact, it had been just over a month, but days of seasickness during a storm had intensified the homesickness we felt after leaving our families. Olive's mother, especially, had clung to her. She feared she would never see her daughter again, for Olive had been a sickly child. Olive reminded her mother of God's promise to be with them even though they would be separated. Finally with the words, "Mother, dear, God has called me; I must go!" she tore herself away, tears stinging her eyes as she walked resolutely up the gangplank.

YES, THE CALL—thrilling, awesome, irresistible! Olive had responded readily. I had responded reluctantly, dragging my feet before making an all-out commitment to the Lord's will. Yet, God had given me some outstanding experiences to draw my attention to His hand on my life.

Born in January 1900 to William and Ada Bolton in Bournemouth, England, the oldest son among ten children, I was slated to continue my father's business. Boltons' Ltd. had begun with assembling, servicing, and selling bicycles, but had progressed to selling motorcycles, and then automobiles. God blessed the business because my father had learned to put Him *first*. "Seek ye first the kingdom of God, and his righteousness; and all these things shall be added unto you," quoted my father. In his business Dad was more concerned about winning a soul to Christ than making a sale.

When the Holy Spirit began to move in various parts of the world at the turn of the century, His moving was misunderstood and opposed by many, but Dad opened his heart and his home. Later, he started a little mission. When he, Mother, and we ten children walked down the street to church, neighbors would jeer: "There goes William Bolton and his congregation!" But nothing daunted Dad. His purpose to serve the Lord wholeheartedly was expressed by his oft-repeated prayer: "Lord, keep us where the fiery fire burns, and in the place where Thou art glorified!"

God did some remarkable things that I, as a young lad, could not overlook. My father, a heavy smoker, was suffering from advanced tuberculosis when he got saved and was miraculously healed. He then began a life of trusting God, even for such things as my sister Vicky's broken finger. It healed instantly! When he prayed for our nearly empty food cupboards, we never ran out of food. Until the age of twelve, I was merely a spectator. But something happened that made me come to grips with God's claim on my life.

Dad and Mother had gone to a prayer meeting one evening, leaving us children at home in the charge of my oldest sister, Winnie. She gathered us together and said, "Let's have our own prayer meeting."

As she told the Bible story I was strangely moved. I slid off the chair and knelt under the kitchen table. It seemed I could see Jesus as He hung on the cross suffering, His hands pierced with nails. When I saw His look of love and compassion for *me* and realized

His suffering was for *my* sin, I wept brokenly, until I knew I was forgiven. I realized the Lord had saved me and I was a new creation in Him. From that day I never doubted my salvation.

There were two great needs in my life, however. For some time I had suffered from an eye condition that left me nearly blind. I had to be led the two blocks to school and could hardly read my lessons. Also, I was very timid and could not speak in public. I was especially afraid to witness to the two boys who lived next door.

The same year I was saved, however, Lily Marshall, a missionary from Egypt, visited our home. She felt led to lay hands on me. The Spirit of God came upon me. I began to speak in another language as in the account recorded in Acts 2:4. What power and blessing I experienced! I forgot about my eyes and was "lost in the Lord" for several hours. When I opened my eyes, to my astonishment I could see perfectly. The Lord had healed me.

The first thing I did after receiving the baptism in the Holy Spirit was to go next door and tell my two friends about salvation. Even though I was ridiculed, this boldness remained with me, helping me to work for the Lord. I began to avidly read the Bible and assist in the mission church by teaching a Sunday school class.

At fourteen I started working and helping with family expenses. Since I had missed so much schooling due to my eyesight, I decided to take night classes in mathematics and engineering. At the same time, because of my father's business, I learned much about mechanics.

God also brought some influential people into my life through the mission. Perhaps the most outstanding of these was evangelist Smith Wigglesworth, noted for his faith-filled ministry. He stayed in our home, and often I would drive him wherever he needed to go. I remember the time a farmer came to him in agitation and asked, "Brother Wigglesworth, do you believe God can do anything?"

"I surely do" was his hearty answer.

"Well, would you please come and pray for my field of cabbages? Caterpillars are killing the whole crop!"

"Of course I will come," the evangelist replied. I drove him to the farm and he prayed over the field, rebuking the devil and his work. The next day the farmer returned excitedly shouting, "They're dead! The caterpillars are all dead! My cabbages are saved, thank God!"

This taught me something about effective prayer. All these things— mechanics included—were preparing me for what God had planned for my life, although I didn't realize it at the time.

Then came World War I. As soon as I turned seventeen I signed up. Almost before I knew it I had completed training for a mechanic in the Royal Air Force and found myself at the front line of battle in France.

The fighting grew worse. And so did the harassment of my buddies who made sport of my religion. Homesick, warsick, pressured to relax my moral standards, I felt my faith was being severely tested. But verses of Scripture and phrases from Christian songs would pop into my mind at the right moment to strengthen and encourage me. Eventually, the buddy who had ridiculed me the most was won to the Lord and became my staunch ally.

I knew my mother was praying for me. "God has a special purpose for your life," she used to say. More than once she had recounted to me the occasion when, as a baby, I was taken for a stroll along a bluff at the seashore. Suddenly, a strong wind blew the baby carriage out of control and sent it sailing toward the edge of a hundred foot cliff. Mother ran screaming, knowing she could never reach the carriage in time. Then, for no apparent reason, it came to a stop on the very brink of the cliff, seemingly suspended in air. "God spared you for a purpose," Mother declared.

God spared my life on other occasions as well. But now in the midst of fighting and death, divine intervention was to be even more dramatic.

While trying to retrieve the precious engine of a plane downed in no-man's-land, two buddies by my side were killed instantly when a shell struck and exploded. Another explosion knocked me unconscious. I came to in a field hospital—in pain and without sight. I heard doctors say I had been blinded by mustard gas.

For the first time, I doubted God's mercy. Had I not served Him faithfully even after entering the armed forces? Had I not endured ridicule and shame for Him? Now my sight was gone. How could I live without my eyes?

But once again I saw Jesus on the cross, as I had when I was twelve years old. His hands left the cross and He reached toward me. I began to realize how much pain and shame *He* had endured for *me.* In an audible voice that I have never forgotten He said, "I have brought you through death. I want you to give Me your life. I need you to carry My message to the ends of the earth."

I said, "Yes, Lord. My life is Yours. I will do anything You want me to do. But what can I do when I am blind?"

"Just commit your life to Me," He reassured.

Suddenly I remembered He had healed my eyes before. He could do it again. As I yielded my life to Him, an ineffable peace flooded my heart; I soon fell into a deep sleep.

After the bandages were removed from my eyes I found I could see. How I rejoiced!

Finally the fighting was over. Peace at last. And I was still alive. I returned home to a joyful reunion with family and friends, intending never to leave again. I became involved in my father's business and found an opportunity to serve the Lord with a group that was taking the gospel to the Gypsies camped near our city. So it was I met Olive, and as we ministered together among the Gypsies we fell in love.

Around this time Mary Lewer, the American wife of Alfred Lewer, an English missionary to China, came to England for a furlough. Her husband had felt he could not leave his work among the tribes in southwest China. After she spoke at our church in Bournemouth about the need for more missionaries, my sister Vicky felt God's call to go. She prayed earnestly that God would provide her passage money and support. And God spoke to a dentist from New Zealand who promised her entire support! Other needs were met in a short time and she was planning to leave for China with Mary.

I, too, had been moved in my heart and challenged by what God had done for Vicky, but I would not let myself be influenced. I told myself I had had a rough time in the war. Now I was getting some attractive business offers. My ambition was to have a nice house and car, to marry Olive, and to settle down. We had our mission field among the Gypsies. The shock came when Olive said, "I can't marry you, Len, if you are going to settle in Bournemouth. You see, I have a call to China."

Oh no! I thought. *First Vicky and now Olive! Surely not Olive!* "You are just overreacting to the talks given by Mary Lewer," I tried to tell her.

"No, Len. God first called me to China when I was eight years old. Now the call has been renewed."

In my heart a conflict began. I felt an aversion to China. But why? Was it because I had heard how my father's older brother, a soldier in the British army, had been treacherously murdered in Peking during the Boxer Rebellion? Or, because some Chinese coolies working on roads in France during the war had stolen and eaten some puppies that were our pets? Whatever the cause, my resistance robbed me of my peace. I did not want to go. I did not want Olive to go. I did not want to be left alone if she went. I was miserable.

Then one night the Lord spoke to me. "What of your promise to Me on the battlefield? Do I and My concern for the lost mean nothing to you?"

I squirmed uncomfortably, remembering.

"This is your last chance," He continued. "If you turn down My call, I'll not speak again."

I could resist no longer. I fell to my knees in the darkness and wept brokenly as my selfish stubbornness melted and my willfulness began to dissolve into His will. What a deep, joyful peace came over my being as I surrendered totally to His will for my life.

The next morning I burned all the attractive offers for business and told my family I was going to be a missionary. Dad had hoped I would take over the family business, but he showed his consecration when he said with deep emotion and a touch of humor, "Well, Vicky is our tithe to the Lord. One out of ten. So *you* will be our offering."

Olive was overjoyed to hear about my decision. But I still wanted personal direction from the Lord as to *where* He wanted me to go, so I spent many hours in prayer.

One night I had a vivid dream. I seemed to see Alfred Lewer

coming to my bedside. "Won't you come and help us?" he asked. "There are hundreds—thousands—that need help and I am the only man here. Won't you come?"

Feeling the impelling force of the Spirit I answered, "Yes, I will come."

He seemed satisfied, and with a smile, turned to leave. "Wait! Aren't you going to stay and see your family and friends?" I asked.

"I haven't time," he replied. "The tribespeople need me so badly." In my dream I saw the lonely missionary walk back across the sea.

When I awoke I had no doubt about where God wanted me to go. Olive was elated, but not really surprised. "I knew it in my heart already."

Mary Lewer was jubilant. "I asked God for three missionaries, and He has answered!" She wrote Alfred, gave us a list of instructions, and then returned with Vicky to China.

Olive and I were married in a beautiful ceremony and had an exciting honeymoon trip on a motorcycle, with a sidecar for Olive.

We began selling our possessions and buying equipment for the field. Dad, together with a few churches and individuals, formed the Tibetan Border Mission. They promised to support us. A letter arrived from Alfred, saying he would travel to Rangoon, Burma, the nearest port, to meet us and escort us to the mission station. He also wrote that we would need £300 ($1,500) in cash on landing. Where would we get so much cash! But, in faith, we sold our motorcycle and bought our tickets to Rangoon.

We were praying, but no money came. Shortly before the sailing date we were at my folks' home when suddenly Dad said, "Oh, I forgot." He reached into his coat pocket. "A lady came into my shop the other day with a serious spiritual need. The Lord enabled me to help her. Before she left she said, 'I heard about your son going to China. God told me to give you this for him.' " Dad handed me an envelope. In it was £300. We were ready to leave! It was September 1924.

PULLING INTO THE DOCK at Rangoon I was brought back to the present by the sounds of a strange, singsong language. Fascinated, Olive and I watched the crowds of coolies in their dark blue pajamalike clothing and pointed hats milling around the docks. My eyes kept searching for a familiar face or the wave of a hand. But there was no sign of Alfred Lewer, or anyone else, to meet us.

Disappointed, we turned to the task of disembarking, thankful, at least, for the kind crewmen who helped us hire rickshas to take us and our goods to the local YMCA. We would just have to wait there until Alfred came.

The excitement of new sights and sounds began to wear off after a couple of days without any sign of Alfred. We began to have strange, new feelings, and struggled with depression. There was the heat, the dirt, the smells. The unfamiliar was losing its charm. We were homesick for England. Where was Alfred?

I found myself pondering this man of whom I had heard so much and seen in a dream. He must be a very likable person. He had been an active member in the Congregational Church in North London when he began seeking the Lord in home meetings with a group of spiritually hungry people. When the Holy Spirit came down in mighty power, Alfred was one of those who was gloriously filled. In the fierce opposition that followed, Alfred was perhaps the only one for whom even the strongest opponents had nothing but a good word. His sunny personality won him friends everywhere. What a good life he could have had back home! Yet he chose to leave it all and identify with primitive tribespeople in a remote area, suffering privations and hardships that few could understand.

Alfred's stalwart wife Mary was no less courageous. From the gentle rolling hills of eastern Pennsylvania, she came to study Chinese in Kunming, Yunnan Province, where she met Alfred. Together in 1918 they tried to open a mission station at A-teng-tze, at an altitude of eleven thousand feet, hoping to reach Tibetans. But as high as it was, the small valley village was dwarfed between two mountains. A-teng-tze represented short days, thin air, bitter cold, and primitive conditions. The Lewers had to retreat to lower ground.

God led them to Wei-hsi where they began to have a fruitful ministry among the Lisu tribespeople. The response was so great that Alfred, Mary, and her sister, Ada Buchwalter, who had come to join them, were not able to minister to everyone. Now the Lord was leading us to join forces with them. What an opportunity it would be to work with and learn from such a man!

But what could be keeping Alfred? I was eager to get started. The journey inland would take many weeks, traveling through rough terrain, cooking our food on the way, and spending nights in crude inns at stopover points. We had been waiting for three days without word from Alfred.

"I think I'll go down to Thomas Cooke & Sons Travel Agency," I said to Olive. "You stay here and rest." She had not been feeling well and we suspected our first child was on the way.

After introducing myself at the travel office, the agent said, "Oh, Mr. Bolton! We have a cablegram for you from England."

With trembling fingers, I opened it. It was from my father. The people at Wei-hsi had sent word to him to contact us. The message said simply:

> Alfred Lewer drowned on his way to meet you. Praying much that God will show you what to do.
>
> Dad

The William Bolton Family in England

Back row: William, Dorothy, Leonard, Winifred, Reginald, Vera, and George (cropped because of photograph's spoilage)

Front row: Olive, Ada (my mother), Victoria, William (my father), and Philip

2

Hands to the Plow

I stood motionless, staring numbly at the words on the flimsy piece of paper in my hand. Alfred Lewer drowned? No! It couldn't be! It must be a mistake. But gradually the fact began to register on my brain. With it came the realization that Olive and I were alone in a foreign country. What now? And what about Mary, Vicky, and the others?

A feeling of heaviness came over me. I walked out into the street thronging with people; never had I felt so alone. How would I tell Olive? She was not feeling well. Could she take it? A dreadful thought came and persisted: *This tragedy has occurred on account of us.* We must be out of the will of God. We should not have come! Now we had better just get passage on a ship and return to England.

Then quietly, insistently, a verse of Scripture repeated itself in my mind: "No man, having put his hand to the plow, and looking back, is fit for the kingdom of God."[1] All at once, I realized this was the Lord speaking to me through His Word. The earlier thoughts had been from the enemy, Satan. My heart was a spiritual battleground. It was Satan who wanted us to go back, to retreat. But did we have any other choice? We had no way to proceed. We did not know the language or the customs. For us, travel in this unknown country without a guide was out of the question. Maps were non-existent. Indeed, what could they record—only trails over range after range of rugged mountains.

But up in those mountains a widow with a small daughter and a baby must be grieving. She was alone except for two women, one of whom was my own sister, Vicky. If I had been needed when Alfred was there, how much more so with him gone! Yet, how could I possibly get to them? There seemed to be no way.

Again God's Word came to me: "I will instruct thee and teach thee in the way which thou shalt go: I will guide thee with mine eye."[2]

By the time I arrived back at the YMCA I knew what my decision must be, but I could not make it by myself. Olive welcomed me with a smile that immediately changed to alarm. "Len, what is it?" she asked.

As gently as I could I broke the news to her. We both wept as we knelt together and poured out our hearts to God, praying for the bereaved widow and for our own guidance. When at last we got to our feet, Olive said, "But we must go on, Len, somehow. God has called us. He will make a way." With that, Olive confirmed my own feelings. The decision made, we again had peace in our hearts.

That night at the supper table an American Baptist missionary, hearing that we intended to travel up-country, suggested, "We're going to Bhamo in a few days. That's up the Irrawady River better than five hundred miles. It's on your way. You could travel with us and stay at our mission station until you have a way to go farther."

We were encouraged and thanked the missionary profusely, realizing that God was with us in spite of tragedy. We sent a message to Wei-hsi, which would have to be carried by a runner most of the way. We assembled our supplies, and were surprised at the amount. But then we had never before had to plan for seven years.

The first stretch of the trip was by train to Mandalay, where we transferred to a river steamer. How thankful we were for the missionaries' help in all the travel negotiations.

Steaming up the river, we were entranced by the patchwork layout of the green rice-fields. Figures in pointed straw hats, ankle-deep in mud, bent almost double, studded the fields. "How beautiful!" sighed Olive. Her sigh changed to a shudder, however, when we stopped at the river ports. Vendors would rush onto the boat with trays of peculiar edibles, calling out their wares through blackened teeth. All the while they chewed some nasty-looking stuff that they would spit on the dock, or even the deck of the steamer— where it looked like blotches of drying blood. "Betel nut," we were told.

"What's the matter, Olive?" I teased. "Remember, you're a mis-

sionary now. You're going to have to forget your nice English ways."
She answered with a surreptitious punch to the ribs. I was glad to
see she was feeling better.

At last we came to Bhamo, which was as far as the steamer could
go. The American Baptist couple offered us accommodations at the
large missionary compound for as long as we needed them.

While our baggage was being unloaded, a Chinese man came up
to me and repeated an obviously well-rehearsed word in English:
"Bol-ton?" Then in Chinese: "Pao Mu-sze?" The man could not
speak English, but something about his face—perhaps it was the
light deep within his quiet, wise eyes—caused me to know he was
a believer.

"Bolton? Yes, I'm Mr. Bolton."

His face broke into a broad smile as he held out a letter. With
mixed feelings of eagerness and concern, I opened it and read:

Dear Pastor and Mrs. Bolton,

This trusty messenger is Pastor David Ho, one of our evangelists. He was accompanying Alfred Lewer near the Tibetan
border when they came to the Mekong River. Since the rope
cable was old they felt they couldn't risk swinging the mules
across the river. Alfred thought he could swim across the river,
leading the animals. Whether a big log or tree hit him or one
of the mules kicked him, we do not know, but David saw him
put up his hands and then go under. His body was found three
days later down the river. David returned the ten days' journey
home and conveyed the sad news to us here in Wei-hsi. After
a few days, we encouraged David to return and try to meet
you in Bhamo.

Now you can trust David with everything, for he is a true
follower of Christ. Come as soon as possible, and bring all the
supplies you can. Change your money into silver dollars if you
can, for we cannot use English currency. May God richly bless
you and protect you on your journey. We will be praying for
you.

With Christian love,
(signed) Ada Buchwalter

P.S. I am enclosing a small vocabulary book to help you with
the Chinese language. It is written in Romanized words to help
you with pronunciation.

What a relief to have received direct word from Wei-hsi at last! Now we had a guide, so we could continue the journey. God had enabled David Ho to find us.

David could not speak English, nor could we speak Mandarin Chinese. The little language book he had brought us was some help: We could point to certain words in English and David could read the equivalent in Chinese. We tried our best to pick up Chinese words, but our success was limited. However, we developed a surprisingly effective manner of communication using gestures, signs, and smiles. A genuine comradeship had begun between national and missionary.

---

[1]Luke 9:62
[2]Psalm 32:8

3

Bandits!

The journey from Bhamo would have to be by mule caravan. We would cook our meals along the trail and camp out at night. Even where there were Chinese inns we would need our own bedding and supplies. We would be exposed to all kinds of weather.

At the foreign exchange I traded our English currency for the heavy Chinese silver dollars. With the help of an interpreter, we hired horses and mules.

As we started packing the mules, one of the bank officials who was watching us said, "You folks are foolish to take all these goods and money up-country into those wilds. There are a lot of bandits in those parts. You'll never get through without losing it all!"

I thanked him for his concern, but explained that the supplies were badly needed by missionaries. As a precaution I interspersed the money throughout the loads. That way if some loads were lost, we would not lose all the money.

Boxes were counterbalanced and attached, one on each side, to an inverted U-shaped frame. Such loads were then placed over specially fitted saddles on each animal. By the time we finished packing we had thirty-five loads. Then, in accordance with their policy, local government officials assigned us an escort of soldiers. Dressed in an odd assortment of faded uniforms and shouldering ancient guns, the soldiers stood in formation awaiting our departure.

Since I had never ridden a mule before, David made sure I had a strong, but well-broken animal. Olive was to ride in a *hua-kan*, a canvas sedan chair strung between two bamboo poles carried on the shoulders of two coolies, one in front and one behind. I marveled at these men, with their calloused shoulders. Thin and wiry, they could walk twenty to twenty-five miles a day on a diet of rice and a few vegetables, with some occasional chicken or pork. I learned that the word *coolie* was derived from two Chinese words meaning "bitter strength."

Before we started out, Olive, David, and I prayed for God's protection. We committed each load to the Lord. All our supplies had come from His hand and all belonged to Him.

At last we were on our way. I was elated, and a little fearful. Despite the slight shabbiness of their uniforms and gear, the soldiers looked brave as they walked beside our caravan. The chant of the coolies, the shouts of the muleteers, and the clatter of the mules' hoofs made a unique background for our thoughts.

According to David's plan, the first day we traveled only twenty miles. My body rebelled at the thought of twenty-one. Dismounting was about all I could manage. David cheerfully explained that I would feel worse the next day, but after the third day the soreness would lessen.

The keeper of the little smoke-filled inn where we had stopped gave us some hot water for tea and David cooked boiled rice and vegetables. After eating, Olive and I spread our bedding on some boards and lay down, too exhausted to worry about the dirt.

The next day we were able to travel twenty-five miles. The trail brought us to the foot of our first mountain range. That night, the innkeeper of the place where we were staying remarked, "How wealthy they must be!" David explained that we were missionaries and had to take inland enough supplies for seven years. The man stroked his sparse beard and told us he had heard that bands of robbers roamed the mountain areas. "In fact," he continued, "some men who had just come over the mountain trail say they saw houses in a neighboring village burned to the ground by the robbers." As David gestured this information to us, apprehension filled my heart.

We had special prayer together before starting our journey up the mountain. Promises from God's Word reassured us:

> He shall cover thee with his feathers, and under his wings shalt thou trust. . . . There shall no evil befall thee. . . . He shall give his angels charge over thee.[1]

It took two days to cross the first high mountain range. At times the path rose steeply and my body ached with the effort of keeping my balance while the mule I was riding climbed upward. At times I dismounted and walked near Olive to encourage and talk with her. A wan smile belied her discomfort.

One morning David came hurrying toward me. Taking me aside, he pointed to the mountains ahead. "Robber, robber!" It was one English word he knew well! My heart began pounding, but I motioned for silence, pointing quickly to the inn where Olive was getting ready for the day's journey. I didn't want her to know the danger that faced us.

A runner had warned the villagers that a band of robbers was approaching. Quickly the people had gathered their valuables and fled. Putting my hand on David's shoulder, we prayed together, he in Chinese and I in English. The God who knows all languages heard and gave peace to our hearts.

"We'll go forward," I said, pointing to the mountain trail ahead. So David gave the order to start. The muleteers were frightened but they gained some assurance as the soldiers shouldered their guns and started marching.

Then we came to a fork in the road. Olive's carriers asked permission to take a shortcut where men's feet could go but not the horses' or mules'. Feeling this to be the Lord's direction for her, I gave my consent. *At least Olive will be safer,* I thought, waving good-bye to her and David, who accompanied her.

The muleteers and I traveled on in silence. Everyone in the caravan seemed to be in the grip of fear. In this jungle territory each bend in the road offered a place of ambush. Suddenly it happened! With ferocious shouts, about thirty wild-looking men came leaping out of the bushes. Our soldier escort turned and fled in panic, disappearing quickly. My heart was in my throat.

The wild, shrieking mob of men were brandishing knives and bows and arrows. Jabbering excitedly, they started beating a couple of the muleteers and unloading some of the mules. I leaped off my mule and, without fully realizing what I was doing, picked up a large stick from the ground. My heart cried out, *Oh God! Help me! We belong to You! This stuff is Yours! You promised to protect us!*

I prayed that prayer in weakness, but suddenly something happened within me. All fear disappeared from my heart. A supernatural surge of power flowed through me. I found myself brandishing the stick and advancing toward the bandits. My voice came forth loudly in a torrent of words I did not understand. I found myself giving orders, using the stick as if it were the rod of Moses.

The bandits stopped dead and stared! They seemed to be listening to what I was saying. I spoke what seemed like a command. Immediately they let go of the mules and boxes. I thundered again, and they dropped their knives and other weapons. Then I shouted something else. With a look of terror, they gave an unearthly yell and fled as though all heaven's legions were after them!

I was awed. God had used the Spirit's gift of tongues to help me. I thought of Moses who had said through the power of God one could "chase a thousand."[2]

Presently, I motioned to the paralyzed muleteers to start moving again. Full of amazement, they reloaded the mules. Not one thing was missing! As they continued the journey, I remained behind until they had rounded the bend. I was experiencing a strange sensation. As the power of the Spirit began to lift from me, I felt as weak as water. I sat down on a rock, buried my head in my arms, and wept uncontrollably—thankful the bandits could not see me now.

Some time later, upon catching up with the rest of the caravan, I was happy to find they had been joined by David, Olive, and her carriers. The muleteers had already enthusiastically recounted to them what had occurred. David and Olive realized this was a miracle of God, and we rejoiced together.

"I almost wish I had been there!" Olive explained somewhat enviously. "I'd like to have seen the devil on the run!"

---

[1]Psalm 91:4,10,11

[2]Deuteronomy 32:30

The Mekong River in Yunnan Province

An escort of hired soldiers with Ada in the background

4

Across the Mighty Mekong

As we continued our journey in upper Burma, terrain would alternate between jungle and mountain. As the blue haze of mountains disappeared, dark green jungle would close about us. Here and there the trail had been tramped by elephants. But usually our muleteers had to resort to machetes, slashing the thick jungle grass to make a way for our party. We camped in small villages or wherever we could find a clearing. Downpours of rain meant wading through swollen streams. Despite the heavy canvas covers over our bedding, rain water had a way of drenching everything.

Finally we reached the great Mekong River in Yunnan Province, China. As I stood on its bank and gazed across its swirling water, my heart started churning. In this river Alfred Lewer had drowned. Why had the Lord allowed it to happen? I had been spared from the hands of ruthless bandits. Alfred had been engulfed in these swirling waters. Weighing heavily on me was the realization that now I—without any knowledge of Chinese ways, language, or customs—would have to take his place. That is, if we ourselves could get safely across. I prayed, "O Lord, please help us!"

Just then an inner voice seemed to say, "I will never leave thee, nor forsake thee."[1] Again God's Word reassurred me.

I saw above me a twisted rope about the thickness of my wrist swinging from a tree and extending across the river. Pointing to it, I looked at David. He shook his head and directed my attention down the river bank. There to my surprise were ten dugouts, each about fifteen feet long, manned by coolies with long poles. The men shouted to us, and we began the steep descent to the brink of the river.

After a long harangue between David and the boatmen, presumably to decide the price of taking across our party, including the thirty-five loaded mules, we were urged to get into the dugouts. Each one was simply a hollowed-out log, its ends built with slabs of wood and the whole affair pitched inside and out with some white substance. I looked at the swirling whirlpools and treacherous currents. Then I glanced back at the caravan. How on earth could these ten dugouts manage thirty-five mules, ten people, and about three tons of goods across such turbulence?

Summoning every ounce of willpower and courage, Olive and I stepped into the first boat. With us came a mule, some bedding, several boxes of goods, and the boatman. The mule wobbled a little on its trembling legs, and then stood quietly, as though sensing it could overturn the boat. "Perhaps he remembers going through this before!" Olive suggested.

The boatman gave an expert twist of his long pole, and without warning, we shot out into the middle of the swirling river. We held each other's hands tightly, feeling sure we were about to share Alfred Lewer's watery fate. The tiny craft spun crazily in the rapids, and then with a twist of his long paddle, the boatman maneuvered the dugout into another current of water that sent us whirling toward the far side of the river. Just as quickly, he braked with his paddle, and we found ourselves approaching the opposite shore.

About the same time, David spun ashore in his dugout, hopped out, and came smiling to meet us. He made motions to explain that since the water was not in flood stage, it was safe for the boatmen to cross. Only in the extreme flood stage was the rope cable used.

We watched as the boats were maneuvered one by one back and forth, bringing the rest of the caravan—mules, boxes, and coolies— across the river. As the last man stepped ashore, we gave grateful thanks to the Lord for His protection. By this time it was evening. It had taken a whole day to cross the river.

David indicated to us that it would probably take only seven more days to reach our destination. This news cheered our hearts.

Our journey took us up through the Mekong River valley. One evening David came into our room in the inn where we were spending the night. He was holding a chicken upside down by its legs. "Pao Mu-sze," he exclaimed, "yu chi!" ("Pastor Bolton, here's a chicken!") We were excited as we anticipated fresh chicken meat. It would be a welcome change from the insipid canned foods we had been eating so long.

David killed the fowl and prepared it carefully for us. To our horror when it was placed before us on a dish, we saw that the meat was an extremely unappetizing gray-black.

"It must be a diseased chicken!" Olive said. And with that she threw it out to the dogs. Seeing this, David became quite agitated, shaking his head in consternation. We did not understand why until much later, when we found out to our chagrin that this special type of black chicken meat is considered the very best, being really tasty!

Once, while traveling single file along a steep mountain pass, one of the mules stumbled and a load of kerosene fell from its back and went hurtling down the mountainside. I breathed a prayer of thanksgiving that it was not one of the more valuable loads and that no lives were lost.

We finally arrived at Wei-hsi, meaning "Western Fort," located near the China-Tibet-Burma borders. This little city, tucked neatly in a fertile valley among several large mountains, was the administrative seat of the county government. As we neared the mud-walled city with its slant-roofed houses, we saw a large group of people coming to meet us.

Pressing through the crowd were the ones we had traveled so far to reach: my sister Vicky, whom I greeted with warmth; Mary Lewer with her new baby, Eleanor, in her arms and five-year-old Katherine by her side; and Ada Buchwalter, Mary's youngest sister. It was a joyful meeting, but heavily tinged with sorrow because of Alfred's untimely death. I was filled with a sense of responsibility toward these women and children: I was the only white man in the area.

Chinese and Lisu believers also welcomed us warmly. It was a time of rejoicing and we felt as if we had known these believers a long time.

---

[1]Hebrews 13:5

Houses of the Lisu people

Wei-hsi, administrative seat of the county government, crossroads of caravans, and eventual base of the Boltons' mission work

5

New Customs, New Language

Olive and I settled in the upstairs of one wing of a large U-shaped two-story building that had been erected by Alfred Lewer a few years before. Ada Buchwalter and Mary Lewer and her two girls lived in another section. Because of the insecurity of the times, we hid most of the silver dollars we had brought. Some we put in a hole in the ground and some in the whitewashed mud walls of the building.

We soon began to adapt to the local customs. The politeness of the people amazed us. Each time believers met us they would bow and express the Christian greeting: "Pao Mu-sze, Pao Sze-mu, p'ing-an!" ("Pastor Bolton, Mrs. Bolton, peace to you!")

At the other side of the U-shaped building was a chapel equipped with a small pulpit and backless benches. How well I remember our first Sunday services there. Fifty or more Chinese children attended, sitting upright and attentive as Ada Buchwalter taught them the Sunday school lesson. In the adult service that followed I was thrilled to recognize the tunes of "Near the Cross," "What a Friend We Have in Jesus," and several other beautiful hymns sung in Chinese. Pastor Ho preached that morning. I was warmed by the fire of God that burned in the heart of this earnest man who had already endured much for the cause of Christ.

Olive and I plunged into the difficult task of studying Mandarin Chinese, the national language. The written language was difficult because of the vast number of characters; the spoken word because of the varied tones. At times I became quite frustrated because so many words sounded the same to me; they were distinguished only by an inflection of the voice and the tone in which they were said. Each word had to be pronounced with the right tone or it would lose its meaning, or worse yet, mean something else. For example, *chu* said with a high level tone means *pig* or *pearl*, depending on the Chinese character or spoken context. However, when said with a descending and rising tone, it means *lord!* In addition to these difficulties, my eyes still bothered me some due to the injury I had received during the war.

Olive was unusually quick. She learned to speak fairly well after only six months of study. She stood on the street and testified of Christ Jesus, the Saviour of the world. Instead of the swarthy faces of the Gypsies back in England, she now faced a mixed crowd of Oriental people: Chinese, Lisu, and even Tibetan.

It took me longer to learn the language. After about eight months' study, I falteringly preached my first sermon in the mission chapel. I spoke about having a clean heart, clean hands, and a clean tongue before the Lord. I noticed some of the people politely hiding smiles behind their paper fans. Later, Olive told me that instead of saying "You must have a clean *tongue,*" I had used the wrong word and preached with emphasis, "You must have a clean *tail!*"

Our instructor in the language, Mr. Lee, was a reserved, scholarly Confucian. For textbooks we used the four Gospels of the New Testament. Mr. Lee was very impressed with the material we covered, having never before come into contact with the Word of God. He would stroke his long thin beard and say, "This *Yeh-su* [Jesus] speaks something like Confucius. He too instructed men to repay evil with good. But there is something deeper and better about the teachings of Yeh-su. Confucius presented the Golden Rule in a negative manner. 'Don't do to others as you don't want them to do to you'; your Yeh-su declares it in the positive."

Mr. Lee began to attend the services in the chapel. We had fascinating conversations with him as we gradually learned to speak Chinese. Over and over Mr. Lee would say, "This verse of Scripture impresses me," or he would ask, "What does this mean?"

He was especially impressed when he discovered the words of Ephesians 4:32: "Be ye kind one to another, tenderhearted, forgiving one another, even as God for Christ's sake hath forgiven you."

"There's no forgiveness such as this in Buddhism or Taoism," he remarked. "There is no doctrine of love in our sacred writings." The Lord used this verse to open his heart.

One day in a gospel service, Mr. Lee responded to the convicting power of the Holy Spirit and openly made a commitment of his life to the Lord Jesus. "I want to give my heart to this God of love," he explained.

Mr. Lee publicly renounced the worship of idols, and we baptized him into the Christian faith.

Although well up in years, he wanted to do something for His Saviour. So he accompanied me on weekly visits to the Wei-hsi prison where he testified to the prisoners.

When his time came, he died a victorious believer.

A Wei-hsi temple

6

The Lisu Respond

Happy as we were for the response among the Chinese in Wei-hsi, our most fruitful ministry was among the Lisu tribespeople.

Ada Buchwalter, already quite fluent in her use of both Chinese and Lisu, had been taking trips into the mountains with Pastor David Ho and some workers to encourage Lisu believers and to evangelize in Lisu villages. She showed remarkable courage in traveling by mule for several days at a time to minister among the tribespeople. One day on returning from a trip, she told us that seventy Lisu in the Ne Bu Lu area had given up their spirit worship, removed all fetishes from their homes, and wanted to be baptized. Would I come to baptize them? The Lisu dialect was new to me, but David and Ada volunteered to interpret for me, so I agreed to accompany them. Olive was not well enough to make the trip.

We traveled by mule through spectacular scenery. Snow draped the lofty mountain ranges, evergreen trees clung to the mountainsides, and gentle breezes hummed a tremulous tune through the pine needles.

As we rounded a bend in the trail, the village of Ne Bu Lu came into view. It appeared to be clinging to the almost-perpendicular mountainside. Coming closer I saw a large chapel built of rough logs. The logs, David informed me, had been taken from a sacred grove of trees where the people had previously conducted spirit worship and danced to demons. Because so many Lisu in Ne Bu Lu had become believers, the grove was no longer used and had been cut down. On that very site now stood this chapel where believers worshiped the True and Living God.

Then we saw the Lisu coming. In single file along narrow trails from different directions they converged on the village. As we arrived they crowded around us. They were barefooted and dressed in homespun hemp. On their heads they wore thickly wound turbans to keep out the cold wind. The women wore thick blouses and voluminous pleated skirts that reached their ankles. Strings of cowrie shells and dried berries adorned their turbans and necks. Many wore silver wire bracelets and large dangling silver earrings. David explained that Lisu men mined the silver in certain areas. These silver ornaments were highly valued and in many cases had been handed down from generation to generation. The men wore loose, nondescript shirts and trousers also made of coarse handwoven hemp.

The lined faces of both men and women reflected the struggle for existence in that rugged mountainous country. Each family kept a few goats or sheep and raised vegetables, mostly turnips, cabbage, and corn. Cornmeal was their chief diet. Despite their poverty, these simple, unpretentious tribesfolk were very hospitable and they possessed a ready, natural humor that enabled them to cope with their dreary circumstances.

I also learned of an oral tradition that spoke of a white man who would one day come and give their people a Book with words of life. Consequently, when Alfred Lewer and his co-workers came and preached the gospel from the Lisu New Testament, it was received with openness. After repenting of their sins, the Lisu turned from their animism (the worship of spirits in rocks and trees) and eagerly received the teaching of the Scriptures.

We now entered the log chapel, decorated for the special occasion with green pine branches and red berries. Pine needles carpeted the earth floor and gave off a pleasant fragrance. The singing began. I was amazed to hear the Lisu believers singing beautifully in four-part harmony.

When David introduced me as "Pao Mu-sze [Pastor Bolton], the new missionary to take Pastor Lewer's place," the congregation rejoiced that the Lord had provided someone to minister as a shepherd to them. But I felt my inadequacy and my heart reached out to the Lord for His help. Pastor Ho preached in the Lisu language, Ada Buchwalter followed with a short exhortation, and then all came forward to pray. They prayed fervently and eagerly yielded themselves to the move of the Holy Spirit.

Then it was time for the baptismal service. We all walked single file down the narrow rocky mountain path to a clear stream dammed up for the occasion. The seventy candidates had been counseled for several months by the church elders. They now stood before Pastor Ho as he exhorted them to take seriously the ordinance of water baptism and truly follow the Lord Jesus. Joy filled their faces as David and I walked into the chilly water. One by one they came forward to be baptized. I had memorized the Lisu baptismal formula. It thrilled my heart as I repeated the words over each of them.

Many of those baptized did not own a change of clothing, so a roaring fire was built near the baptismal site. Immediately after being baptized they ran quickly to the fire to warm themselves and to dry their clothes. I was told that many of them had never before had their whole body immersed in water, yet now they had been willing to venture into the cold stream to show publicly their commitment to Christ.

After a time of singing and praising the Lord around the fire, we returned to the chapel to partake of the Lord's Supper. As the bread and grape juice (which we had brought with us) were passed around reverently, the believers wept with joy and gratitude. I observed tiny pools of tears on the floor where the people fervently worshiped the Lord. Then as the Holy Spirit came upon them they glorified God and spoke in other tongues. I was amazed to hear one man say in English, "Jesus is coming!"

By this time it was evening. Village women prepared a supper. Men brought long tables and benches out of their huts and placed them end to end. There in the light of pine torches and wood fires, we enjoyed fellowship with one another and the kind hospitality of these Ne Bu Lu believers.

That night, as I lay on bedding spread out on hard boards in a smoke-filled hut, I prayed, "Lord, make me a spiritual father and leader among the Lisu." Even as I prayed myself to sleep, I could hear their melodious voices singing songs of praise.

The next morning we held a dedication service for the new log chapel. I preached a simple message in Chinese, interpreted by David into the Lisu dialect, and encouraged the congregation to use their chapel for the glory of God and to dedicate their bodies to the Lord as temples of His Holy Spirit.

David then gave the Lisu believers an opportunity to testify. A man rose. "You have no idea," he said to the visitors, "of the change that has come since the message of Jesus was brought to our village. We know Christ saves! Before, we were always drinking, fighting, and even killing one another with the big knives we carry. Then we heard of God's love. Now we are living in peace, like brothers and sisters. God has transformed us by His power!"

Several testified of healing. After we had prayer together we dedicated children, together with their parents, to the Lord. Family after family filed past Ada, David, and me, as we laid hands on them, claiming them for the Lord.

After a couple of days in Ne Bu Lu it was time to return to Weihsi. We shook hands with over two hundred believers as they filed past us, many with tears in their eyes as they bade us good-bye. We assured them of our prayers and encouraged them to be faithful and true to the Lord. As our small caravan of mules rounded the bend in the mountain trail, we could still hear the echo of their voices as they sang:

> *Till we meet, till we meet,*
> *Till we meet at Jesus' feet,*
> *God be with you till we meet again.*

In my heart, I knew that we *would* meet again.

Ada and her children surrounded by believers in the village of Ne Bu Lu

Lisu tribesmen

7

Hour of Darkness

The time was fast approaching for the birth of our first child. We had decided to travel downcountry to a China Inland Mission (CIM) hospital located in Ta-li. We had written to the supervisor of the hospital, Dr. Hanna, an American physician, to inform him of our coming. My sister Vicky felt led of the Lord to accompany us; Olive would need plenty of help. We took only a few mules in our caravan because we planned to return shortly after the baby was born.

Olive was transported in a *hua-kan,* the Chinese sedan chair. She looked pale and wan. Every evening during the journey, Vicky and I prayed earnestly that the Lord would strengthen Olive.

Our route, which was new to us, took us across the high Li-ti-p'ing range and then down a long valley where a tributary joined the great Yangtze River. We traveled three days along the Yangtze. During our journey we seized opportunities to give gospel tracts to people. At the dirty inns, we sat around the evening charcoal fire and witnessed to the people of Christ's saving power. However, we did not find these Chinese people as responsive to the gospel as the Lisu. They would politely nod their heads and take our literature, but they were aloof to the message.

At one point in our journey, a small band of men suddenly appeared in the distance, fired two shots in our direction, and yelled for money. As usual, our escort ran away. The narrow path at this point skirted a precipice. I said to Vicky and Olive. "You both sing the chorus 'Under the Blood, the Precious Blood.' " As they started to sing I rode ahead on my mule. Then around the bend came about twenty bandits, rolling two large millstones down the trail straight for us.

While we continued singing, I brandished a stick in my hand.

Then in the name of the Lord, I threw the stick at the leading millstone. As it struck, the millstone veered, crashed over the precipice and down the side of the mountain. And the second millstone followed the first!

I dismounted and started preaching to the robbers. I rebuked them for their wicked ways, their acts of plundering, stealing, and killing people. The Lord gave me the right Chinese words to speak. I further explained that we were not wealthy people and that in our party was a woman who was soon to have a baby. Not one of the men dared to look me straight in the eye.

I then told Vicky, Olive, and the muleteers of our caravan to pass by. Upon seeing my pale wife in the sedan chair, the robbers seemed to soften in their attitude—they even bid us good-bye as we left them!

Less than a mile up the trail we came upon a horrible sight: people whom the bandits had killed or wounded. Those who were still alive cried out for help. We did what we could, administering first aid and sending for help.

The ten days of travel were wearisome, especially since I could see Olive was suffering. I would ride beside her sedan chair and try to encourage her as we traveled along.

Eventually, as we neared Ta-li, we sighted the beautiful Erh-hai Lake glistening in the sun, sampans dotting its shining surface. I gasped at the beauty of the scene. Even Olive's eyes brightened as she strained to see the view. High above its shoreline we followed the road along the long, narrow lake. Tucked in the valley was the large walled city of Ta-li, its Moslem pagodas, built centuries before, guarding the area like sentries.

"It won't be long now, darling," I reassured Olive. "We'll have you in a nice clean bed, and you'll be comfortable and under the care of a good doctor."

Our caravan clattered through the city gate and up the cobblestone street to the CIM compound. There a hearty welcome awaited us. I helped Olive out of her sedan chair and into the hospital. Vicky and I were given rooms in the mission house. Nearby stood a large stone CIM church.

The following day, Dr. Hanna called me in for consultation. "Pastor Bolton, I'm sorry to tell you this, but there's a serious problem because your wife's body is so small. I am concerned for her life as well as that of the child."

I grasped his arm. "But doctor, isn't there something you can do? She's all I have!"

The elderly doctor was kind as he put his hand on my shoulder. "Of course we'll do all we can," he said. "But I'm afraid there are signs of dropsy also."

Vicky sensed my anguish and again we united in prayer.

The next day Olive started in labor. I stayed by her side hour after hour and held her hand to reassure her. Suddenly she quoted faintly: " 'Though I walk through the valley of the shadow of death, I will fear no evil: for thou art with me.' "[1]

I tried to comfort her. "You'll be fine and deliver a healthy baby boy!" She smiled fleetingly, a faraway look on her face.

Then I was asked to leave. I waited in my room. The hours dragged by.

Then a sudden knock on my door startled me. "Pastor! Come quickly!" The servant's voice was urgent. I ran to the hospital room. Dr. Hanna stood by Olive's side. "She has delivered a baby boy," he said, "but she hemorrhaged a great deal and she's very weak."

I looked anxiously at the colorless face. Presently she opened her large blue eyes, and with just a glimmer of a smile upon her lips, said, "I'll see you, dear, in glory." With a faint sigh she closed her eyes and was still.

"Olive! No!" I cried in panic: "Olive, you can't go! We've just begun—You can't go! Oh, no!" But she was gone. I dropped to my knees, sobbing. Wave after wave of agony poured over me. Was there to be no end to the sacrifice? First Alfred, now my own wife!

Vicky hastened to my side. After a few minutes she gently pulled me to my feet. "Len," she said, "the Lord wants her more than you do. Come, let's see the baby." I seemed to be in a dream as my sister led me down the corridor to another room. There I looked at my firstborn son, a tiny wisp of humanity. He looked blue and near death's door.

"Is he all right?" I asked numbly.

The doctor, looking exhausted, came to my side. "Pastor Bolton, we had a terrible struggle. We did all we could to try to save her! Perhaps we can save your baby, but I'm afraid he has a weak heart."

"It's better if he's taken too, since his mother is gone," I said bitterly, with the sorrow only a young husband can feel.

"Come!" said Vicky. I leaned hard on her strong young arm as she led me to my room. All that day I lay on my bed unable to move; the suffering of my heart overwhelmed me.

Why has God done this? Why did He call me to China only to lose my wife, the darling of my heart? These and a thousand other questions burned in my head.

That evening Vicky urged me to take a little nourishment. Then Dr. Hanna informed me the baby had expired. I felt numb, floating around in a consciousless void. Vicky and several CIM missionaries gathered around me and prayed, but I seemed beyond the reach of God or man.

Because there was no way to embalm bodies, missionary friends held the funeral the next day for both mother and son in the CIM church. Outside the walled city was a foreign cemetery surrounded by an iron fence for keeping out wild animals. In a daze, I found myself taken out of the city in a ricksha to this cemetery. Dr. Hanna himself conducted the committal service. When the coffin was lowered, I wanted to throw myself into that gaping hole and bury myself with my wife and child.

Vicky stayed by my side, a tower of strength in that black hour. She took me by the arm and led me back to the mission compound. "Olive's safe with the Lord Jesus," she said. "Her troubles and trials are over. Now you and I have a work to do. Think of Wei-hsi and the thousands of Lisu up in the mountains."

I scarcely heard a thing she said. Her words had no meaning for me. Several days went by. I was still in a daze. Then one morning, I rose from my bed and slipped away for a walk. I came to the city wall and climbed up the steps on its inward embankment, then walked the well-worn path along top that went around the city. I looked at the curved tile roofs of the houses on one side and the rice paddies with the lake and mountains in the distance on the other side. The beauty of the scenery moved me somewhat, and I felt a little lifted in spirit by the sunshine. I walked on and on.

As evening shadows began to fall, gloom once more settled over me. I stopped and looked over the outer edge of the wall with its sheer drop of over fifty feet. Suddenly, the enemy seemed to whisper to me, "Why don't you just end it all? It's not worth the sacrifice! Throw yourself down from the wall and end all your misery."

Looking over the edge, I noticed the vines and wild flowers hanging precariously from the stones. Then, as I stepped closer, another voice clearly spoke: "I gave *My* Beloved for you. Can you not give *your* beloved for Me?"

I broke before the Lord. His promises poured into my aching heart like soothing oil: "I will never leave thee nor forsake thee[2]. . . . Have I not promised? Be strong and of good courage! . . . Rise up and possess the land!"[3]

A stream of comfort and courage began to rise up from deep within my being until it became like a rushing river. I sat down on a large stone and wept like a baby, with healing tears of release. "Thank You, Lord! Thank You for bringing me to my senses. You are worthy of any sacrifice. I will trust You to help me. You will never leave me nor forsake me!"

As I began to praise the Lord, a miracle took place in my heart. New strength flowed into my soul. I felt like a new man. The power of God surged over me like a mighty torrent. I began praising the Lord and speaking in another language given to me by the Holy Spirit. My spirit experienced release and victory. This time the very legions of Satan fled—like so many Chinese bandits.

Vicky was amazed at the change in me. Before, I had been a brokenhearted, defeated man; now she saw courage and light in my face. I had met with the Lord and He had given me victory. She praised the Lord and we worshiped Him together. The sorrow and loneliness were still there, but so was the Comforter. Later I received a letter from a woman in England. During those dark days she had spent an entire night on her knees in prayer "for the Leonard Boltons." And the Lord had answered.

I started moving like a new man, making plans for the journey back to Wei-hsi. Vicky and I thanked the CIM missionaries for all their help and comfort, then we left Ta-li and traveled north.

Ten days later we crossed the lofty Li-ti-p'ing range and descended the winding trail down the mountainside. Great masses of pale green moss clung to the giant trees around us. Then in the distant valley we saw the familiar city we called home.

Ada and Mary met us with Lisu and Chinese believers at the river below Wei-hsi. We wept together over Olive's homegoing, but they were relieved when I made known my resolution to remain with them and carry on the work of the Lord.

---

[1]Psalm 23:4
[2]Hebrews 13:5
[3]See Deuteronomy 1:21

The Li-ti-p'ing mountain range near Wei-hsi often crossed by the Boltons

Loading up the mules

Travel by *hua-kan* (sedan chair)

8

New Vision, New Venture

Olive's death closed a chapter in my life, but opened an aching void. By filling my days with feverish activity, I tried to forget. Although I had accepted Olive's death and I felt no rebellion against God's will, questions remained. They would shoot through my mind like sharp-pointed arrows, especially in the darkness of the night. The death of Alfred had been shock enough. But now the death of my wife and firstborn son! Was there to be nothing but death? I seemed to see it all around. It was in the faces of the heathen people. Death and darkness—spiritual darkness.

Then a verse of Scripture came to my mind, "Watchman, what of the night? The watchman said, The morning cometh."[1] I believed the Lord wanted me to be a faithful watchman in the night, to warn the unconverted of their ways and to persuade them to turn to God in repentance and faith.[2] For the morning follows the night! Once more I had heard God's message of hope and promise. In the words of the hymn:

> The long, long night is past,
> The morning breaks at last, . . .
> The Comforter has come!

As the Holy Spirit, the Comforter, again filled my heart with the presence of the Lord, the haunting questions no longer seemed to matter.

One day five Lisu men came into the mission compound with news of sixty more people in Lisu country who were ready to be baptized. Would we come? When David asked me to go with him I leaped at the opportunity.

We wanted to travel light so we prepared only two mule loads:

one with our bedding, cooking utensils, food supplies, and clothing; and one with Lisu gospel booklets, songbooks, and gospel tracts. Then, mounting our horses, we took leave of my sister Vicky, Ada, and Mary.

The five men, now our escorts and guides, were excited about our willingness to accompany them to territory that was new to us. We climbed over two steep mountain ranges. After three days' journey we reached our destination, the village of La Pa Shan, perched on the precipitous slope of a mountain. Lisu believers came out to meet us with gifts of chickens and eggs. One family sacrificed their only full-grown pig to provide us with pork. Such was the kindness and hospitality of the people.

I was thrilled as I saw God's grace at work among these tribespeople. So many of them had turned to Christ. Desiring a place of worship, the believers had cut down trees and constructed their own chapel from rough-hewn logs, similar to the one I had previously visited at Ne Bu Lu.

That evening we enjoyed a service in the newly built chapel. When David and I examined the candidates for baptism to see if they understood the step they were taking, I was amazed at their knowledge of the Scriptures. Their elders had done their work well, instructing the believers and encouraging them to memorize God's Word. Some of the young men had often sat up late into the night studying and memorizing the Scriptures by firelight.

In the Lisu log cabin where we were to spend the night I was directed to spread my bedding upon a long wooden box. As I lay down to sleep, I was horrified to discover the box was a coffin. When I objected to David, he nonchalantly replied, "Never mind, Pastor Bolton, there's no one in it." He then explained that it was customary for a family to purchase a coffin ahead of time for an elderly father or mother, who liked the security of knowing it was ready when he or she needed it. It just so happened to be ready when a missionary also needed it—as a bed!

Early the next morning the whole village was astir for the important activities that had been planned. First was the pigtail cutting ceremony. Pastor David Ho produced a large pair of shears. The men lined up and he proceeded to cut off their pigtails. Their long braids had been a sign of subservience when China was ruled by an emperor. Now that the country had become a republic, the believers felt they no longer needed to wear this symbol of bondage.

The Lisu women were especially happy for the Christian message. "We were taught that we were just like cows," they told us. How grateful they were to learn that they had souls like the men and Christ had included them in His great plan of salvation. They loved to hear the stories of Hannah, Ruth, and particularly Mary Magdalene, out of whom the Lord cast seven demons and who was the first to see the risen Christ Jesus.[3]

We all gathered at a nearby stream where the water had been dammed up for the baptismal service. David and I baptized the sixty candidates. Many young people were baptized as well as the old and feeble. One convert was a young mother who had given birth to a baby just a week before.

After the baptismal service we returned to the log chapel for a Communion service. Then followed the dedication of babies, and finally, with great rejoicing, the dedication of the chapel itself. This undoubtedly was a highlight in the lives of these villagers.

Believers gave us eggs and chickens in return for the Lisu gospel booklets and songbooks we had brought with us. How happy they were to get them. Paying (that is, trading) for the literature made it mean more to them.

So many people gathered for the service that evening, the elders decided to make a large bonfire and have the service outside. Over the sound of crackling logs, I preached in Chinese with David interpreting. Wolves and jackals howled occasionally in the distance. Overhead a myriad of brilliant stars twinkled. What a moving experience to see those weather-beaten faces in the light of the bonfire and hand-held pine torches drink in the truth of God's Word! Their fervent singing penetrated the stillness of the night, the gentle wind carrying the sound far into the pine-covered mountains about us.

Before the night was over, however, black clouds moved in and soon it poured down rain. We dived for shelter in a little log cabin with about thirty other people. Since the roof leaked, David and I set up umbrellas over our bedding in a corner. We tried to get some rest, but we slept very little—the Lisu believers continued to talk and sing, fellowshipping through the night.

When the next day dawned clear and bright, we began our homeward journey, rejoicing in the wonderful things that God, through His Holy Spirit, was doing among the Lisu tribespeople. As I ventured forth in ministry, I was being renewed in my own life.

---

[1]Isaiah 21:11,12
[2]See Ezekiel 33:7-11
[3]See Mark 16:9

Victoria (Vicky) Bolton

Leonard Bolton

9
Wei-hsi Clinic

Back in Wei-hsi I continued to study the Chinese Mandarin language. Finding it difficult to stick with the lessons and books full time, and seeing people come to the mission compound with various kinds of ailments, I decided to start a clinic on the premises.

For those seven-year terms of frontier living we had to have all kinds of supplies to make us nearly self-sufficient. The Lewers had told me before leaving England to bring a full range of tools: gardening equipment, leather goods and tools for repairing shoes and saddles, and a range of medical supplies. It was to the medical supplies that I now turned.

My first patient was a big Tibetan. Tibetans were often seen in Wei-hsi for it was a crossroads of Tibet, Burma, and China. Long caravans with products of fine Tibetan rugs, sugar (in rock form), and butter frequently snaked their way through the narrow streets of Wei-hsi. My Tibetan patient had a swollen jaw due to an infected tooth. I took a pair of dental pliers, and—without anesthesia of any kind—pulled out the offending tooth. So grateful was my patient that he gave me a large chicken, which he pulled from inside his homespun tunic much as a westerner would his billfold from inside his suit coat.

People came to our clinic with skin, head, and stomach ailments. We gave worm medicine to poor little children whose stomachs were bloated from parasitic worms. We had quinine for malaria, aspirin for fevers, antiseptic liquid and petroleum jelly for sores. In addition to administering medicine, the lady missionaries and I prayed for those whose ailments were beyond our simple remedies.

Once I was asked to treat a teenage girl whose father had knocked out her tooth and dislocated her jaw. I looked desperately in my medical book for directions. Then, protecting my fingers from her sharp teeth, I wrenched her jaw and heard a click as the bones slid back where they belonged. She shook my hand and cried in gratitude. Her mother gave me a dozen eggs in payment. I witnessed to the family about the Saviour and they promised to attend gospel meetings at the mission chapel.

Another case was a girl who had been kicked by a mule. She had a huge gash on one side of her head. I gathered my medical supplies and hurried to the house where the family members were wringing their hands in despair. The poor girl was bleeding profusely. First, I applied pressure above the wound, stopping the flow of blood. Then, using a needle and thread, I sewed the skin back together and applied antiseptic ointment to the wound. A few days later the mother came to our mission compound with tears of gratitude. I told her to thank the Lord God of heaven and gave her some gospel literature.

One night I was in bed reading when I was interrupted by an urgent knocking. I hastily dressed and went downstairs to the door. A man with a torch in his hand pleaded, "Please, foreign doctor, come quickly. My sister has taken too much opium and is dying." Grabbing my medical kit, I accompanied the man to the house. I learned that his sister had been told by her parents that she would have to marry a man she detested; she had tried to commit suicide. I gave her some medicine to induce vomiting. Then I reasoned with her parents until they agreed to reconsider their unfair demand. Later, the girl came to the chapel services; she had the shine of the Lord Jesus on her face.

What had begun as a diversion from language study became a means of preserving physical life and introducing spiritual life. I realized the Lord was working through my amateur medical efforts. After having grappled with death, I felt this ministry was therapeutic. But God also had in mind a broader purpose.

10

Out of Revulsion—Love

One day three Tibetan men came into the Wei-hsi mission compound and asked to talk to the foreign pastor. These travelers had come from La-p'u, a village located near a famous lamasery (Tibetan Buddhist monastery) five days' journey away. In the exchange of greetings the visitors startled me by sticking out their tongues at me! I soon learned this was the customary Tibetan greeting.

The men had first heard about the gospel through a medical missionary, Dr. Albert Shelton, who served under the Foreign Christian Missionary Society (Christian Church). (Tragically, Dr. Shelton was later shot by bandits in Tibet.) The visitors begged David and me to bring the good news to the people in their area.

I was interested in learning more about these burly Tibetans. Then, too, my sister Vicky and I were currently serving under the Tibetan Border Mission (TBM). The incentives being strong, I readily accepted the invitation.

Some Tibetans could read Chinese, so David and I took a large supply of Chinese Bibles and hymnbooks. And since we would be passing through Lisu country, we also packed Lisu literature. Mary urged me to ride Jerry, her strong, reliable mule, which she had ridden on many trips up-country. "Jerry seems to know the trails in those remote areas," she said. "He has more than once saved the caravan from getting lost."

Other mules were hired to carry supplies and literature. Saying good-bye to the women, we started on our evangelistic trip. We rode up one steep mountain range after another. On the third day we lost the trail. Soon it became dark. I was learning, as had the Lewers in their experience at A-teng-tze, that darkness descends quickly when it's aided by the long shadows of high mountains. I grew somewhat apprehensive and swung off my saddle to be on foot. David lit his kerosene lantern, an invaluable item on trips, and we struggled on in the dark. In the distance wolves and jackals howled, their strange cries echoing in the night. I held on to the tail of "faithful Jerry," hoping Mary was right about his knowing the trails.

She was! Around midnight we saw a welcome sight—men bearing pine torches coming toward us. They were Lisu Christians looking for the lost travelers. Since David and I had been on the road for over fifteen hours, we were quite happy to reach our destination among the Lisu. The villagers exclaimed again and again, "We're so glad you have come to teach us the Book!" A steaming meal of rice, meat, and corn had been prepared for us. Eagerly our Lisu friends gathered around, inviting us to eat.

I immediately attacked some of the big chunks of meat served with the rice. Suddenly I stopped, looking questioningly at David. He laughed at my expression. "What kind of meat is this?" I asked.

"Monkey meat."

I prayed to the Lord to help me eat it, knowing that it was considered a breach of etiquette to refuse food. Being very hungry helped.

With our appetites satisfied, we placed our bedding on large boards in a log cabin, slung up our mosquito netting, and soon fell asleep, utterly exhausted.

The next morning I awoke to the sound of singing. David was already teaching the young people choruses and songs from the hymnbooks we had brought. They asked eagerly for copies, giving in return eggs, corn, or millet. We stayed several days, holding services and instructing villagers in the truths of the gospel. About twenty people found Christ as their Saviour. Older men in the group were appointed elders to help watch over the new converts. Then we left to continue our journey, promising to return the following year to give the converts further teaching and baptize them.

We journeyed on to Tibetan territory, in high altitudes where few trees grew. Herds of yak dotted barren mountainsides and wide plateaus. Well suited to the high altitutes and the harsh climate, the yak resembled a small buffalo.

The Tibetans rode the yak, milked the yak, and ate the yak. They used its fur for boots and clothing (the fur facing inside) and its dung for fuel. They even used its butter as a kind of human insulation, smearing it over their bodies. (Because the Tibetans normally never took a bath from birth to death their odor could be quite overpowering.)

At last the La-p'u monastery came into sight. One of the Tibetans in our small caravan knew the head lama (priest), and through him we gained entrance into the temple precincts. Inside, red-robed lamas with shaved heads chanted rituals. A huge golden Buddha occupied the chief place in the large room. Incense smoke filled the air. Illumination came from yak butter lamps suspended from the ceiling.

After the chanting ceased, the lamas welcomed us and asked us to be seated. A servant passed around a large bowl to each guest. I asked David, "What kind of soup is this?"

David replied, "It is Tibetan tea with yak butter. The hot drink will do you good!"

As the bowl of brown liquid was placed in my hands as a gesture of hospitality and friendship, I noticed some hairs floating gracefully on top, along with a chunk of yak butter—and even a few lice. The rancid odor of the butter made me feel sick. I watched David drink from his bowl, slurping as though he enjoyed it! I realized that I, too, must drink from mine; to refuse would seriously offend our hosts.

Desperately, I prayed two prayers: first, after blowing off some of the top layer that included the hairs and lice, I said, "Lord, thank You! Help me to accept their hospitality and to drink this stuff"; then, after gulping most of it down, "Lord," I pleaded, "help me now to keep it down!"

The head lama, a huge man, greeted us by bowing low, sticking out his tongue, and putting up his two thumbs. We bowed low in return. David addressed him through our Tibetan friends. Then David presented a copy of the Tibetan New Testament to the head lama, holding it in both hands and bowing low. The lama also bowed and received it with both hands. Then he began to finger it curiously.

The head lama and his colleagues probably had never before seen a white man or this strange book. They asked many questions: "From where does the white man come?" "Why have you come?" "Who wrote this book?" "From where does it come?" "What does the book teach?"

David seized the opportunity to explain the gospel very simply to them. However, their interest was superficial.

The more we conversed the more we realized a barrier stood between us. Although their religion demanded extreme dedication and rigorous asceticism, spiritual darkness prevailed. The lamas we saw there were firstborn sons who had been given by their parents to the cause of Tibetan Buddhism. They would spend their lives in prayer, meditation, memorization of their sacred texts, and chanting rituals. The only change from this routine would be when they roamed the area outside begging for alms, and when they participated in the devil-dancing celebrations, wearing grotesque masks.

We watched the lamas whirl their prayer wheels containing written prayers, which they believed would ascend to their deities as the wheel revolved. Their religion consists of building up merit through incessant prayers, celibacy, repetition of chants, and performance of rites. In this manner they seek a state of illumination that Buddha himself is said to have attained. At the end of many cycles of reincarnation lies the highest goal: *Nirvana,* a state of utter extinction, illustrated by the flame of a lamp being blown out.

The show of hospitality completed, the lamas returned to their mournful chanting, accompanied by the occasional beating of a large drum hung on ropes from the rafters. They were repeating the phrase, "Om Mani Padme Hum!" ("Honor to the Jewel in the Lotus!") I learned this was an utterance of praise to "Lord Buddha." I watched one lama bowing to the ground in worship until his forehead bumped on a stone before the idol Buddha. The continual repetition of this act of obeisance had formed a large callus on his forehead. Our presence had already been forgotten.

As we turned to leave, my heart was heavy. *Can these men ever*

*be freed from this spiritual bondage? Oh, that they would discover
life and light in the Lord Jesus Christ!*

As we left this famed lamasery we saw vultures hovering overhead.
The sickening, rancid smell of butter-smeared bodies lingered in
my nostrils. To this was added the stench of dead bodies. David
explained that Tibetans often place their dead on the lamasery roof
where vultures pick the flesh from the corpses. They believe that
the souls of the deceased are helped by the birds as they ascend
skyward, to heaven—only to be reincarnated again.

We took the path down the mountain to La-p'u to spend the night
in the dirty inn. But I could not sleep. The Tibetans in this area
appeared to me even more filthy than any of the Lisu I had met.
Having been raised in a home,where cleanliness was taught as being
next to godliness, I was now being affected by the accumulation of
all I had experienced. A revulsion was rising up and growing stronger
within me, undoing all the progress I had made in adjusting to the
cultures. I felt myself drawing back, not wanting to mingle with
these people any more. But how could I minister to the people
when I felt I could never love them? Praying desperately, I cried,
"Lord, help me!"

That night the Lord spoke to me in a dream. I saw a filthy individual standing before me, draped in an assortment of rags. Everything about him was repulsive. I exclaimed, "This must be one of
the filthiest persons I've ever seen!"

Then the Lord Jesus spoke softly, "Leonard, that is how *you*
appeared in My sight. But I loved you when you were unlovely. I
left the ivory palaces of glory and came down to earth. I died on
the cross for you. Before My precious blood was applied to you,
you were just as unclean as any of these people who have never
washed. But I loved you. Can you not love these less fortunate
people for Me?"

Then I awoke. This experience made me realize how inadequate
was human love and how much I needed God's love. I bowed my
head humbly before the Lord and asked forgiveness. As I prayed,
I experienced a baptism of love; His love was shed abroad in my
heart by the Holy Spirit. From that time on my attitude changed
completely. God gave me such a love for the Tibetans and the Lisu

that I was able to eat with them, sit with them, sleep in their homes, and accompany them for days at a time. Out of my revulsion the Lord planted His love.

We visited some homes while in La-p'u, but had little response; the people there seemed bound in their spirits to the lamasery. They would take their offerings of food and money to the lamas; in return, they depended on the lamas for the salvation of their souls. Only a few consented to buy copies of the Tibetan New Testament. David and I prayed that the seed of the gospel would eventually find fertile ground and bear fruit.

We then headed southward toward the Yangtze River to evangelize in Chinese towns that had never heard the gospel message. Where we could, we strung large chorus sheets between two poles or trees. I played my concertina to attract a crowd. David taught choruses from the song sheets, pointing out the Chinese characters one at a time with a rod. He and I took turns preaching briefly, using large Chinese art posters depicting some Gospel narrative or parable. Then we appealed to listeners to put their trust in the Saviour, the Lord Jesus. Here and there a few responded. Some literate men leafed through and bought copies of the Chinese New Testament. To the women, children, and elderly, who could not read, we gave gospel picture cards, which they eagerly received.

Before returning to Wei-hsi, we visited Chu-tien, a town located by the Yangtze River. When curious onlookers gathered in the marketplace we preached the gospel to them. They had never heard the good news, or "happiness sound," as it translates in Chinese. How David and I prayed the Lord would send messengers and establish a church there! In time, the Lord answered our prayers. The Howard Osgoods from America, and later the Oscar Sierings from Germany, established a Pentecostal church at Chu-tien.

After two more days of travel, once again crossing the high Li-ti-p'ing Mountains, we finally arrived home.

While David and I were away, Mary, with her baby Eleanor and little Katherine, Ada, and Vicky had traveled to Ne Bu Lu for a Bible study convention at the invitation of Lisu leaders. They had loaded up a folding organ, food supplies, and bedding, and ridden by mule.

Over a hundred Lisu leaders and believers had attended, crowding out the log cabin. So, true to our experience, some of the sessions had needed to be held outside, around a roaring fire. The people had listened attentively to various Bible studies given by the ladies. Ruth Ho, David's wife, had interpreted the studies into Lisu. As the people had gathered day after day for the Bible teaching, prayer, and preaching services, the blessing and inspiration of the convention had increased. Everyone, especially the new believers, had enthusiastically enjoyed the fellowship.

The concluding night, as the Lisu believers had wended their way home, Mary had exclaimed, "What a beautiful sight! Just look at the pine torchlights flickering all over the mountainside and down in the valleys! These Lisu are leaving with not only their pine torches, but also the gospel torch to light flames all over Lisuland!" Her comment proved to be prophetic.

Missionaries at Wei-hsi: Clifford and Lavada Morrison with Baby
Lyonel, Mary Lewer with Katherine and Eleanor, Vicky and
Leonard Bolton

"The Tibetans rode the yak, milked the yak, and ate the yak."

David Ho preaching in the open

Tibetan lama with his rosary (Notice the bump on his forehead.)

11

Out of Terror—Romance

It was the year 1926 and the Communists were gaining power under the leadership of one Mao Tse-tung. Communist bands, or "Reds," as they were known then, roamed the lands. They would clash with the official government (Nationalists) for the next twenty-three years.

With political unrest, banditry increased. Since Wei-hsi is located at a crossroads of several trade routes, robber bands were a constant threat during my first term as a missionary. Chinese warlords vied with each other and overtaxed the common people on the pretext of protecting them.

We missionaries were wondering why we hadn't received any mail from England or America. Upon inquiry, we learned that bandits had been robbing the mail carriers and seizing all our letters and parcels, sometimes killing the mail carrier. This time of anxiety brought our little group together in fervent prayer. We sought the Lord to protect us and to bring important mail through. The Lord didn't fail us; we were never in want of basic supplies.

Then one winter we heard the infamous bandit leader Chang Chi P'a and his men were joining forces with another band of robbers to attack Wei-hsi. So terrifying were the rumors that we were advised to hide our silver money. Our Lisu friends offered to take some of our valuables to their villages to protect them.

The bandit leaders sent a message to Wei-hsi officials demanding surrender or they would burn the city to the ground. They had already robbed the towns of Chu-tien, along the Yangtze River where David and I had preached, and Lu-tien, closer to Wei-hsi. Word came that they were planning to cross the Li-ti-p'ing mountain range and attack Wei-hsi the following day.

This was frightening news. I called together believers in Wei-hsi: David and his wife Ruth (now pregnant), some Chinese believers, some Lisu leaders, and our missionary group. This latter group included Clifford and Levada Morrison, recent arrivals to study the Lisu language. Conscious of the imminent danger we earnestly sought the Lord. The Lisu pastors, too, were concerned about their villages and chapels; they knew the bandits would stop at nothing in their plunder and slaughter.

As we prayed together, the Lord gave us wonderful peace and assurance that He would take care of us. His promise came to us so clearly:

> He that dwelleth in the secret place of the Most High shall abide under the shadow of the Almighty. . . . Thou shalt not be afraid for the terror by night; nor for the arrow that flieth by day.[1]

While we were praying, the Lord sent a silent but powerful deliverer in the form of tiny snowflakes. The storm lasted for three days, covering the Li-ti-p'ing mountain range with six feet of snow. The bandits' plans were foiled and they were compelled to turn eastward toward Tibet. God had protected us. We rejoiced and praised the Lord for answering our prayer.

We were to see God at work in a different manner some time later. Government soldiers were locked in deadly combat with the armed bandits who were seeking control of the whole northwestern part of Yunnan Province. They were plundering every town in their path, leaving such suffering and destruction that the whole area was in a state of chaos. A runner who escaped brought the news to Wei-hsi that another band of robbers was headed in our direction. The Wei-hsi county magistrate warned us to escape into the mountains with the Lisu believers. But we felt the Lord wanted us to stay. Once again we gathered for prayer in our chapel.

That evening I returned to the house on an errand and, on impulse, went out onto the upstairs veranda. From there I could see beyond the city wall and over the countryside. Just then, Ada came out onto the veranda and, seeing me there, joined me. We looked out into the distance where the smoke and lurid flames rose from a village that had been attacked and set on fire.

"What a dangerous situation we are in," I ventured. "I have a message here from the robber chief stating that if I use my hunting gun against them they will burn down the mission station." I showed her the letter in my hand.

She looked at it. "Perhaps they should be more concerned about a stick in your hand."

I looked at her then, and to my surprise her eyes held no fear. What a missionary she was! Such faith! Such bravery—going out alone with the nationals, riding mules on trips in the mountains that would daunt a strong man! Then my thoughts shifted and I became aware of how feminine she was, how truly a woman. I looked into her eyes as she glanced up at me. Her fair hair shone in the moonlight. All at once I was filled with love for her.

"Aren't you afraid, Ada?" I asked softly, using her first name.

"No, Leonard, I'm not afraid." It was the first time she had used my first name and it thrilled me. "The Lord will take care of us."

"I would like to help Him take care of you," I said on an impulse, taking her soft hand in mine in the darkness of that danger-filled night. Downstairs in the chapel the believers were singing, "Under the blood, the precious blood." When she did not rebuff me I leaned down and gently took her into my arms, feeling a rush of joy when she yielded to my embrace.

"Ada, I love you!" I found myself saying. "I want you to be my wife. Will you?"

She nodded her head, eyes downcast. Tenderly, I tilted her face upward and kissed her. All danger was forgotten as we pledged ourselves to each other. The moment was ours alone. We felt instinctively that God wanted us together, to unite in our service to Him.

Just then Mary called, "Ada, where are you?" and the spell was broken.

We rejoined the others in the chapel and continued in prayer into the night. David whispered to me that the magistrate had sent some local soldiers to fight the bandits. Soon we heard the sounds of battle as the bandits neared the city walls. We heard screaming, rifle shots, the zing of arrows from bows, and the sound of men shouting. About three in the morning it became quiet. The battle had ceased. But we continued in prayer until daybreak.

The next day, the official opened the city gates and commanded his servants to pick up the wounded. Since our mission compound was near the city gates, he asked if they could bring the casualties to us. Our mission was turned into a hospital as wounded bandits and soldiers (we didn't know one from the other) were brought in. The women quickly tore up sheets and other clothing to make bandages and I grabbed my medical bag. There were men with gaping head wounds, broken legs and arms, and mangled bodies. For hours, David, Clifford, and I washed their wounds, cleaning them with antiseptic, and set their broken bones. We stitched up the wounds with needles and thread and administered help wherever we could.

Divine energy and wisdom were given us during that time of acute need. As we looked over the dead and wounded, we found not one believer had been injured or killed! Because of the help we were able to give, the official was profuse in his thanks. He felt our prayers had helped his soldiers overcome the bandits. We heard later the bandit leader had realized he was outnumbered and retreated. He and his men went eastward, never to bother us again. Once more Wei-hsi was saved.

The next day, the magistrate sent a messenger for me to come and "heal" his horse just as we had his soldiers. When I entered the official's compound, I found his fine white horse lying on its side, a huge gash in its rump six inches above its tail. I felt it was impossible to help the animal and told the official he should shoot it; otherwise it would bleed to death.

"No," he replied vehemently. "You didn't shoot those worthless soldiers. You did your best to fix *them* up. You fix my horse!"

It was a command I dared not disobey. I hurried home and returned with a sacking cloth needle, tough string, and wire pliers. I asked some soldiers to tie the horse's legs together so it couldn't kick and to sit on its head so it couldn't bite. Then I went to work. With the large needle I stitched the flesh together, pulling the string through with the pliers. The horse twitched and writhed under me, but with tremendous effort, I put five large stitches in its rump.

After applying antiseptic to the wound I went home. I tended it for ten days, watching to make sure there was no infection. Then the horse stood on its feet and started to swish its tail.

The magistrate looked at me and his face beamed. "Hsieh, hsieh, Pao Mu-sze!" ("Thank you, Pastor Bolton!")

In light of all these events I now understood the "wider purpose" God had had in mind for the Wei-hsi clinic.

By this time, most of the soldiers were able to go home. Some of them were scarred for life, but they were thankful to be alive. The magistrate was also thankful—for the life of his horse as well as his soldiers. He invited all the missionaries to a feast at his mansion. At long black-lacquered tables, seated in straight-backed chairs, we were served a twelve-course meal. Along with the usual dishes of chicken, pork, and fish, we were served the special delicacies of black pickled eggs, buried in the ground for over a year, shark fins soup, and fried bees.

"You eat the bees like you eat the pork fat," the magistrate explained to me as he politely used his chopsticks to place the juicy morsel in my bowl.

Ada and I had decided not to make our engagement known to the national co-workers until we had made further plans. But the feast we enjoyed at the magistrate's home seemed like an appropriate celebration of our newfound happiness—a romance that came into being during a time of terror.

---

[1]Psalm 91:1,5

12

Ada Buchwalter

With a new zest for living I now allowed my heart and mind to dwell on the remarkable woman who had consented to be my wife. Appreciation of her character deepened into an admiring love. And what joy to know that she returned my love! Yes, we could both work so much better together. God was good! As I learned more about her fascinating background I could trace the hand of God in it all.

Ada's parents, Martin and Lydia Buchwalter, were prosperous farmers in Paradise, Pennsylvania. They were direct descendants of Huguenots who had escaped from the province of Alsace, France, in 1685 during the extreme religious persecution of those times. One of their ancestors was Isaac LeFevre. When he was sixteen, his parents, five brothers, and a sister were murdered by Roman Catholic authorities. He escaped to the home of friends in Strasburg, Germany, carrying with him a large loaf of bread into which his mother had baked their French family Bible. Later he fled to Batavia where he fell in love with and married Catherine Ferre, also a Huguenot.

Befriended by Queen Anne of England, the family migrated to London. There they heard about the freedom to worship God in the new land of America. Madame Ferre, Catherine's mother, went in person to the sympathetic William Penn, who consented to sell them a two thousand acre tract of land near the town of Lancaster, Pennsylvania. Queen Anne granted them permission to colonize in the New World.

Isaac and Catherine LeFevre, their small son, and Catherine's parents, the Ferres, arrived in America in 1708. At first they stayed with relatives near what is now Kingston, New York. Then in 1712 they traveled to their destination, about sixty miles west of Philadelphia. Arriving late one summer afternoon and seeing the peaceful, picturesque valley, they named the place Paradise.

Settling there was not without excitement, however. One day Catherine was terrified when she suddenly encountered a burly Indian in his feathered headdress. To her surprise and relief he said in broken English, "Me no hurt white woman!"

Isaac prospered in his new homeland. To the day of his death he cherished the Bible that had been saved from his father's home in France at the cost of his family's lives. That copy is now preserved in a museum in Lancaster.

In the sixth generation after Isaac LeFevre, Ada's mother Lydia was born. Married at sixteen to Martin Buchwalter, she had two sons and four daughters, of whom Ada was the youngest.

When Ada was seven, an epidemic of diphtheria swept the countryside and many children died. Ada herself came down with a severe case of the disease. The doctor's diagnosis was very grave. He gave her an injection of antitoxin, which was experimental at that time. Despite this treatment there seemed to be little hope. However, after a month, with prayer and her mother's careful home nursing, Ada began to recover. The Lord had spared her.

The family now were Mennonites. Lydia Buchwalter herself wore the customary plain black ankle-length dress and black bonnet until the day of her death. But she was open-minded enough not to stand in the way when her children were drawn into a revival movement that was sweeping the area. It brought unexpected changes to this quiet Mennonite family.

WHEN ADA WAS ELEVEN YEARS OLD she watched enviously as her sisters and brothers loaded up camping equipment and went with her father to a Christian and Missionary Alliance camp meeting at Rocky Springs, near Lancaster. Her mother thought she was still too young to go. The following year, however, Ada persuaded her mother otherwise. She enjoyed the revival singing and testimonies, the Bible teaching and preaching (under such men as Dr. A. B. Simpson), and even prayer for the sick! For the first time she was exposed to missionary speakers telling how the Lord was working in other lands. She felt convicted of her own need of the Saviour.

One evening after a Spirit-anointed message, when the altar call was given, she stepped out to give herself to the Lord. It was a wonderful conversion! Two days later she was baptized in water. As she came up out of the water she saw a glorious sight: a shining path right up to heaven! A deep yearning was born in her heart to point others to that shining path.

Although such education for girls was frowned upon by their Mennonite neighbors, Ada was permitted to take four years of high school at Wilson Memorial Academy in Nyack, New York. There her sister Mary was attending a related school, the Alliance Missionary Institute.

About this time God was pouring out His Spirit on seeking believers in various parts of the world. A move of God took place also among the students at Nyack that prompted Mary to really seek God. That summer, after an all-night prayer meeting during a Rocky Springs camp meeting, she received a glorious baptism in the Holy Spirit. Following that she received a distinct call of God to take His message to China. Mary had visited a Pentecostal church in Newark, New Jersey, pastored by Rev. Allan Swift, where a remarkable, continuous revival was taking place. This had a profound influence on the direction of her life, and, in turn, on Ada's.

One night as Ada lay sleeping, Mary quietly entered the room, laid her hands on her sister, and prayed, "Lord, baptize Ada in the Holy Spirit, and give her a call to China." Not having awaked, Ada did not learn of her sister's prayer until later.

Not long after this, Ada felt a compulsion to visit the church in Newark, even though it meant traveling alone by train for over a hundred miles—quite a challenge after her sheltered upbringing.

She arrived at the address just before dark. To her dismay the door was locked and no one was around. Alone on that city street, she did the only thing she knew to do—pray! Soon a young man came along. When she asked him about the church, he exclaimed, "Praise the Lord! Now I know why I felt compelled to come back here to stoke up the furnace now rather than after the service! The church has moved to a location nearby and we are using this old one as a dormitory for some of the fellows who are attending the services. Come, I'll take you to the new place."

They arrived at the church and Ada thanked the young man profusely. Upon entering the building she was struck with an awesome awareness of God's presence. She felt a joyous anticipation combined with a deep reverence. Ada had always been a "good girl" but now in His holy presence she began to realize the sinfulness of sin. Everywhere in the building people were being affected as they yielded to the moving of the Holy Spirit. Conversation was centered on the Lord Jesus, the wonderful Saviour. Ada was thrilled by the singing in the Spirit, which she had never heard before. God's Word came alive under anointed preaching. Her heart melted before the Lord.

Seeking the Lord required determination and perseverance. On the third day while she was praying quietly at the altar, it seemed the fountains of the deep within her were opened and she began to praise the Lord in a voice that almost frightened her. Praise poured forth from her lips and she began to speak in a strange language. Joy filled her soul. Then it seemed the Lord was speaking to her, asking her if she was willing to go to China for Him, to carry the gospel to people there. She hesitated, and the power of the Spirit lifted.

The following day a few of the ladies went with Ada upstairs where they waited before the Lord. Again the Lord began to deal with her about China. Somehow she felt she would lose the lovely sense of His presence if she were not willing to obey Him. She yielded and said, "Yes, Lord. I'll go to China—*with You.*"

Joy flooded her soul, and she burst out in another tongue (in a Chinese dialect, a missionary told her later). It was exhilarating! It seemed as if she were living in heaven for about a week; she didn't care to eat or drink. Feasting at the table of the Lord, she felt no need for physical nourishment.

After her return home, Ada had a special visitor. Ben had been a classmate at Nyack and they were practically engaged. Ada had written him about the baptism in the Holy Spirit, including Scripture references for him to look up. Now he had come to tell her he could not accept it and to ask her to recant.

"How can I deny something that is so real and important to me?" She exclaimed. "If you would only believe, you too could have this blessing." He stiffened and said, "You will have to make a choice between me and this 'baptism.' If you won't repudiate it, then our friendship must terminate!"

"Then terminate it must!" Ada answered. God was now first in her life.

It was not easy to watch him leave, but later she was glad, realizing that Ben would not have been the right one for her.

God had been working also in the lives of Ada's brothers and sisters. Her older brother Reuben, having received the Baptism himself at Newark, began prayer meetings in his home and subsequently also at Lancaster. This led to the establishment of a Pentecostal church in that city. Another brother, Omar, and his wife also took part in these activities together with Mary and Ada. This Lancaster church later became a staunch supporter of Mary and Ada's missionary ministry.

In 1914, Mary left for China. Her parents were reluctant to see her go to "the ends of the earth." They had prayer and wept together as they surrendered their dark-haired daughter to the Lord.

When Ada told them that she too had a call to China it was doubly difficult for them. But she promised to wait for God's time.

Ada found daytime employment at the Watt & Shand department store in Lancaster, but she put her best energies into the fledgling church: cleaning the rented hall, making the fire, playing the pump organ for the services, and sometimes leading the singing. Wherever she could she witnessed to people about salvation.

In the summer of 1918, the Lord confirmed to her that she should start preparing to leave for China.

Many of the revival groups had come together to form the Assemblies of God. Ada heard that the annual gathering of the General Council would convene in Springfield, Missouri. She felt the Lord was directing her to travel there and ask for appointment as a missionary. Then she would have the backing of a mission board and financial help could come through churches rather than just from individuals. As if to confirm her conviction, the Lancaster church offered to send her as their delegate to the General Council sessions.

She was quite nervous as she came before the Foreign Missions Committee in Springfield. Two men, Rev. Robert Brown, pastor of Glad Tidings Tabernacle in New York City, and Rev. Joseph Tunmore, an executive in the Eastern District Council of the Assemblies of God, recommended Ada to the brethren. To her joy she was accepted for appointment and became one of the early missionaries sent out by the Foreign Missions Department.

Special words of encouragement, along with her first missionary offering, came from Rev. Stanley Frodsham, editor of a weekly that later became the *Pentecostal Evangel.* His wife Alice had also attended the school in Nyack, New York.

Ada was asked to participate in a great rally that brought before the people the church's responsibility to take the gospel to the world. From that time offerings began to be sent for her support as a missionary.

Everything was not full of promise, however, for she became very ill upon her return home. Ada's father had died a short time before and her mother was clinging to her, the only daughter left at home. Her mother could not accept Ada's going to China. She thought of Ada's illnesses and her many allergies. Seeing the sorrow in her mother's eyes, Ada experienced an intense struggle. *Shouldn't I stay with her until she too passes on?* she wondered.

Then the Lord gave her a passage of Scripture:

> Hearken, O daughter, and consider, and incline thine ear; forget also thine own people, and thy father's house; so shall the King greatly desire thy beauty: for he is thy Lord; and worship thou him.[1]

At the same time the Lord spoke to Ada's mother. He told her that if she did not truly consent to her daughter's leaving, He could simply take Ada to heaven. Ada's mother yielded, helping to sew some of the clothes Ada would need.

The Lord healed Ada and provided the supplies she would need to take to China, where she planned to join Mary. At her farewell in the Lancaster church, the pastor and deacons dedicated her to the work in China; then a brother laid his hands on her and prayed a unique prayer in simple eloquence: "Lord, do not allow any disease to touch her body while in that foreign land." His prayer was marvelously answered. In forty-six years of foreign missions service, although she had minor mishaps, Ada never once contracted a disease!

The day came when a little group of loved ones and friends gathered at the railroad station in Lancaster. Ada's heart was breaking as she said good-bye, especially to her mother, but God's call was stronger than the ties of home. A poem rang through her mind:

> *Let me hold lightly to temporal things,*
> *I, who am deathless, I who have wings!*
> *Let me hold fast, Lord, to things of the skies!*
> *Quicken my vision, open my eyes!*

IN APRIL 1919, WITH A TRAVEL COMPANION provided by God, Ada set sail for China from Vancouver, Washington. Enroute they stopped in Japan. Seeing the teeming crowds, Ada marked that as her first taste of the Orient. Three weeks later they sailed into Hong Kong. Looking down at the hundreds of little sampans bobbing in the harbor waters, Ada was astounded to learn that families called such cramped quarters home. On the way to the mission home in Kowloon they were jostled by the crowds of people and all kinds of hand-pulled vehicles: rickshas, carts, wagons, wheelbarrows.

Ada saw people everywhere, absorbed in a myriad of occupations, jabbering in a frighteningly strange tongue (Cantonese, she soon learned).

Then she waited for direction from the Lord about her next step—arrangements for inland travel. Five years earlier when her sister Mary had arrived in Hong Kong, the Lord had guided her with a challenging article by a missionary, Grace Agar. She had written about the open door among the tribal people in Yunnan Province in southwest China. Traveling companions were provided unexpectedly when the Allan Swifts, who had left their church in Newark, New Jersey, to go to China, arrived in Hong Kong. They, too, planned to go to Yunnan Province; Mary was able to travel the long journey overland with them. *Will God do the same for me?* Ada wondered. She was to travel to Kunming, the provincial capital, where she would stay at a missionary home for language study before joining Mary, who by now had met and married Alfred Lewer.

God did not fail Ada. She met a nurse who was also looking for someone with whom to travel. Together they prepared for the trip as well as they knew how. The women went by ship to Haiphong, six hundred miles. Then, limited to daytime travel only, they endured five hundred thirty-five miles by train—tunnel after tunnel, bridge after bridge, with breath-taking precipices in between.

Each time the train stopped they were besieged by vendors shouting their strange wares, not realizing they didn't understand a word. Ada was horrified at their red-black, betel-nut-stained teeth and their coarse manners and unkempt appearance. With dismay she thought, *Is this what the heathen are like to whom the Lord has called me?* Then she reasoned with herself. *These people are not really Chinese; they are French Indo-Chinese. When I get among the Chinese I will feel different.*

Finally they arrived at Kunming, the capital city of Yunnan Province. If she had been shocked by the Indo-Chinese along the way, she was altogether unprepared for what she now faced. She and her companion were mobbed, pushed, and jostled until finally, with relief, they recognized the missionaries who had come to meet them. The missionaries claimed the women's baggage, then shuttled them through the crowd to the rickshas for a ride to the missionary home.

Ada found her first ricksha ride fascinating, if not altogether pleasant. After she climbed into the chair-like two-wheeled vehicle, a coolie, dressed in what looked like a pair of black pajamas, picked up the handles and pulled her along. He had a filthy sweatcloth draped around his neck; as he ran he would wipe his perspiring face. A strange smell filled Ada's nostrils as she was wheeled over the cobbled city streets. Later she found out that no sewer system existed, other than open drains, and the smell was of human excrement being taken out of the city in buckets to fertilize the fields. "Honey buckets" was the nickname used by the missionaries.

Multitudes of people were walking on the sidewalk and in the street. Nevertheless, the coolie picked his way nimbly through the crowds, skillfully dodging pigs, dogs, and children as he went. Finally, to Ada's relief they arrived at the Pentecostal missionary home where she was welcomed by Rev. and Mrs. Allan Swift and other friends.

Ada was given an upstairs room with a good view of the city streets. The calls of the vendors drifted up to her room constantly throughout the rest of the day and night. As she lay awake on her bed that night she was conscious of her mixed feelings: homesickness for her loved ones, fascination with the Orient, and anxiety about the future. On a sudden impulse, she climbed out of bed, knelt down, and poured out all her doubts and fears to the Lord. Gradually, a sweet peace filled her heart as God reaffirmed the call He had given her. Ready to love the people, however unappealing they seemed at present, she climbed back into bed and slept like a tired child.

Studying the language was grueling and frustrating. Ada battled to make her American tongue and lips form the baffling sounds and difficult tones of Mandarin. Her teacher smelled of garlic and knew no English. Ada prayed for grace as day after day she bent over the books and drilled, drilled, and drilled again. Soon the day came when Ada addressed an audience for the first time, in morning prayer at the mission compound. Then came the children's meetings, conversation in the market, and finally, after a year's hard work, the big final examination. She passed.

ADA HAD RECEIVED LETTERS FROM MARY describing the vast areas with no gospel witness. Mary had also written of the difficult conditions with which she and her husband Alfred struggled, especially the getting of proper food for them and milk for their new baby boy. They were planning to leave A-teng-tze, on the Tibetan border, to seek a less hostile environment.

Just before Ada's language study was completed, another letter arrived. Mary wrote that baby Alfred had taken ill with pneumonia. They had prayed desperately for his healing. Then one night, as they were praying, he threw up his little hands and went to be with Jesus. They buried his tiny body under the ice and snow. Then they moved to Li-chiang where they would stay with some Dutch Pentecostal friends, the Klavers, to rest and await Ada's arrival.

It was a bad time to travel. Bandit activity in many areas had intensified. Travelers were being harassed. The doctor who had delivered Mary's baby (Albert Shelton) would be shot by bandits only a few miles from his home. But Ada's concern about the welfare of her sister compelled her to face these dangers.

Because attacks were being aimed at missionary men who could be held for ransom, it was not considered wise for Alfred to come all the way to Kunming to meet Ada. He sent two young tribal men to escort her from Kunming to Ch'u-hsiung where he would await her arrival.

Ada gathered her baggage and hired carriers and mules to start her first journey inland. A missionary from the Netherlands, Miss Bakker, would accompany her part of the way. Missionaries in Kunming prayed for them as they left. One of them insisted that Ada take a box of insect powder and keep it handy. She thanked the missionary, but didn't give it much attention.

They had traveled about ten miles the first day when a message came from a government official, ordering them to stay in a nearby town while he assembled an escort of soldiers for their protection on the way.

Then came Ada's first night in a Chinese inn. Closing her eyes to the dirt, she spread her bedding on the boards and hooked up her mosquito net. Soon, however, her eyes came wide open. Although her two young escorts had locked her in to keep her safe, she had intruders. They came in force, boldly, in single file along the string of her mosquito net, tiny flat red creatures—bedbugs! Now was the time to give grateful attention to the insect powder thrust upon her by the thoughtful missionary.

She was awakened early the next morning by the loud raucous sound of the clearing of throats and spitting, the customary procedure on starting a new day. Later, as they assembled their small caravan, to Ada's astonishment they were joined by a contingent of several hundred soldiers. She felt like the prophet Elisha surrounded by horses and chariots of the Lord.

It took them six days to travel to Ch'u-hsiung. Riding a horse was new to Ada, but for enjoying the scenery she decided it couldn't be matched. They climbed narrow trails over mountains, forded streams, and crossed stone bridges. In the deep gorges beautiful orchids hung over the rocks, and ferns and flowers grew everywhere. As they crossed the plains in the warm sunshine, the rhythmic ring of the horses' hoofs and the chants and calls of the horsemen put her into a state of daydreaming. Suddenly her horse turned, sending her over his side and into a patch of stinging nettles. The daydreaming ceased.

With a heightened awareness of the horse beneath her, Ada continued the journey. Unfortunately she communicated her newfound awareness to her horse, which, she thought, became just as nervous as she. Approaching a bridge having a deep drop on one side, the horse seemed to swing too close to the edge. To compensate, Ada instinctively leaned to the "safe" side of the horse. The lean turned into a fall. This time there were no bushes to break her fall, only rocks. She suffered two broken ribs.

Someone procured bandages—the type of white cloth strips used to bind young girls' feet to restrict their growth—and Miss Bakker wrapped Ada's chest. Thus supported, she felt there was nothing more to do but mount her horse again, with help, draw strength from prayer, and press on toward Ch'u-hsiung. In this condition Ada met her brother-in-law Alfred for the first time. He welcomed her warmly.

After a few days of rest and hospitality in the home of Miss Morgan, an American missionary who had founded a Christian school in Ch'u-hsiung, Alfred hired a *hua-kan* for Ada and they journeyed for ten days to Ta-li. It would take another five days to reach Li-chiang where Mary would be waiting. Three days after leaving Ta-li, they saw in the distance some people waving to them. Mary, her co-worker Ruth, and several other believers from the mission had come part way to meet them. After a separation of six years, it was Ada's coming to foreign soil that brought about a joyful reunion.

Seeing Ada's improvised cast, Mary asked, a twinkle in her eyes, "Are you trying to set a new style of dress?"

"Don't make me laugh—it hurts!"

What hurt more than Ada's ribs, however, was her sister's loss of her baby. After arriving in Li-chiang, the two sisters had time alone in the mission lounge. Ada listened to Mary's full account of her baby's death.

"Why did the Lord take our precious baby boy?" she finally asked. The bitterness was unmistakable.

Ada sat helpless, not knowing what to say. Then, on impulse, she went to the organ. Accompanying herself she sang softly:

> *O sweet wonder, O sweet wonder,*
> *Jesus, the Son of God.*
> *O how I love Him, how I adore Him,*
> *Jesus, the Son of God.*

The Name that we proclaimed for the conversion and comfort of the pagan was equally efficacious for the needs of His children. Mary began to praise His name. Tears trickled down her cheeks as peace flowed into her heart. They were both wonderfully comforted by the unseen but real presence of the Lord.

---

[1]Psalm 45:10,11

13
Mission Base: Wei-hsi

Li-chiang was only a temporary home for the Lewer missions party. After much prayer about the right place to settle, God laid Wei-hsi on their hearts. Ada seemed to feel a special burden for this strategic city, located at the crossroads of several caravan routes.

Before settling there, however, they made a survey trip on horseback of the surrounding areas, evangelizing in the towns and villages they came to.

One centrally located town was Lan-p'ing. Arriving just at dusk, they spent the night in an inn. Very early in the morning they awoke to find the room filled with thick, acrid smoke coming through cracks in the floorboards. People in the rooms below had kindled wood fires for cooking. The missions party felt like smoked hams! Quickly folding their cots, they hastily exited down the rough stairs and into the open.

They conducted brief street meetings in Lan-p'ing. Ada played her Autoharp to attract a crowd, and they sang from the large song sheets. On the theory that even a nominal price exacts more appreciation than no price, they offered gospel booklets at a small price. Several people bought copies. As Ada, Alfred, and Mary answered questions and explained about Christ, a few accepted Him as their Saviour. One woman wept as she was told the story of Jesus. The Lewer party felt privileged to be the first to preach the gospel in an area rarely traveled by Westerners.

Their outreach continued into ten surrounding villages. A woman received Christ and burned all her idols, and several young girls also believed.

At the village of La Chi-ming, they met an old man who had heard the gospel twenty-five years earlier from a CIM missionary.

He invited the Lewer party into his house. Another woman gave them vegetables and listened intently to the message.

Upon returning to Lan-p'ing, they claimed the town for God and prayed that someone might come to continue evangelistic ministry there. Some years later my sister Vicky, after marrying Harry Fisher during her first furlough in England, went with him to Lan-p'ing and established a church there.

After three more weeks on the trail, following the route of the Mekong river, the small missionary group finally reached the top of a mountain range. And there, far below, nestled in the valley, was the walled city of Wei-hsi. The magnificence of the view was breathtaking. Their trail zigzagged down the steep mountainside until it reached the valley floor. As they gazed enthralled at the verdant valley with its winding river, a tributary of the Mekong, the Lord confirmed His word to them that they were to claim the area for His kingdom. They were exhilarated.

By the time they had descended the trail and entered the city, night had fallen. They had traveled from the heights into the depths. Bone weary, they found their way to an inn and roused the reluctant innkeeper. They had to sleep on the wooden floor with only a few travel rugs because their goods had not caught up with them. During the night they noticed an unpleasant odor and heard strange sounds. The following morning they discovered their room was over a pig-pen! Cobwebs festooned the rafters and dirt covered everything.

As was the case throughout the region, the people were unaccustomed to seeing white people; they considered the missions party a great curiosity. Crowds assembled for the street meetings.

Before the Lewer party settled fully, however, they made a trip to Li-chiang for the birth of Mary's second baby, Katherine. Alfred then returned to Wei-hsi to prepare living quarters. Mary and Ada followed when the baby was ten weeks old. The rainy season had begun, making it a difficult trip. Instead of six days, it took them two weeks to reach Wei-hsi.

Ada, Alfred, and Mary made their home in an old house Alfred had rented, covering the soot-blackened walls with pages from a Montgomery Ward's catalog. When it rained, the roof leaked copiously; they would protect their beds with yellow oil sheets. A second house not far away was rented and fixed up for a chapel.

Children began attending first and were quick to learn the songs and Scripture verses. God began to work in lives. One boy hurried home to his mother one day. "I'll do anything you want me to do," he said, "except one thing. I don't want to put incense sticks before the idol on the godshelf. I have learned from the pastor at the Happy Sound Hall that Jesus Christ is the Son of God. He is the Living God, not made of wood or stone."

The mother listened. The Holy Spirit began to work in her life, too. Later, she opened her heart to the Lord and accepted Christ. She burned her idol and even offered a room in her house for gospel meetings. Her son later took the name of Peter and attended our short-term Bible school. Subsequently he went to help in the mission at Lan-p'ing and became a co-worker of the Fishers.

Many other children wanted to follow the Lord, but were forbidden to do so by their idol-worshiping parents. However, among some adults who were converted was an influential woman, Mrs. Chao. After receiving the baptism in the Holy Spirit, she became a radiant witness and influenced others to turn to Christ. This nucleus of believers formed the beginning of the Wei-hsi church, the first in the whole area.

It was at this time that Mary left with young Katherine for England and the States for a much-needed furlough—and recruitment of help. Alfred, who felt he could not leave the work to go with them, moved to live upstairs above the chapel. He and David Ho preached the gospel in other villages. Ada also traveled to the mountain villages, accompanied by Ruth, and later, after their marriage, by both Ruth and David.

The response among the Lisu tribe was such that the small missionary party could not keep up with all the calls for them to minister. No wonder, then, that they were overjoyed at the news from Mary that she had prospects of *three* new missionaries joining forces with them. They were my sister Vicky, and my wife Olive and I.

Alfred then leased property and began construction of a mission house. The compound, located by the city wall near the west gate, became a God-given blessing. Alfred, however, did not live to see it fully developed. The U-shaped building housed the chapel in the wing nearest the street gate and living units for missionaries on the other two sides. Near the chapel were living quarters for Pastor Ho's family and other nationals who came in from time to time. The mission station had a stall along the back wall for milking cows, a long coop for chickens, a vegetable garden, and some fruit trees. Especially necessary in those days, rooms for traveling missionaries and guests were also a part of the compound. For example, the Clifford Morrisons first lived there while in language study, before going on to the Salween River area.

But most important, the mission compound provided a home base from which we could reach out to the surrounding country and to which believers could come for teaching. And how they did come!

Building the mission house at Wei-hsi

Project completed (The chapel wing is out of sight on the right.)

14
Joining Forces

The year was 1927. Ada had been in China for eight years without a break and badly needed a rest and change. My furlough would not be due for another three years. We decided, therefore, that she should take her furlough now, going first to England to meet my family, then to the United States. On her return trip I would meet her in Hong Kong where we would be married. Then, together we would continue our work in Wei-hsi.

After a wistful farewell, she started out with David and some helpers who would go with her into Burma as far as Bhamo, after which she would continue on her own. It was an eventful journey. Many times upon arriving at a village at evening she learned that bandits had left just that morning. However, the Lord took her safely all the way to Rangoon where she boarded a steamer for England.

Uneasy about meeting her future in-laws alone, Ada felt my father broke the ice when he welcomed her at the Bournemouth railway station with a hearty hug. And her charming ways, American though they were, soon found an opening into all of their hearts.

Invitations to speak came from many churches, even from as far north as Scotland, where the renowned speaker and writer Rev. Donald Gee pastored a church in Edinburgh. People sponsoring the Tibetan Border Mission wanted to hear about Olive, Vicky, and me.

After crossing the Atlantic to America, Ada had a joyful reunion with her dear mother and other relatives. As she ministered in her home church in Lancaster, the Lord moved on people to dedicate their lives to God, resulting in at least one young man, Lester Eisenberger, becoming a pastor.

Meanwhile in Yunnan, the political situation was going from bad to worse. An antiforeign feeling was spreading. Chinese warlords were rising and falling. In this state of civil war and the resulting lawlessness, bandits were about in force. The British and American consuls requested the evacuation of all missionaries. On the national scene, President Chiang Kai-shek was fighting the Communist forces that had fled to Kiangsi Province and now were heading farther west toward Wei-hsi. We were virtually isolated and ignorant of these conditions.

One evening I was preaching in the chapel when a runner breath-lessly interrupted the service with the message that missionaries were ordered to flee the country immediately; their lives were in danger. Some Americans had already been killed in Nanking. The earlier warnings had failed to reach us.

We held a hasty conference and made our plans. I would wait in Wei-hsi until two Dutch missionaries, Miss Scharten and her friend, could come from Li-chiang to join Vicky and me. We would then travel together over the regular route, dangerous though it was, to Bhamo and then to Rangoon.

Mary opted to leave with her two daughters and join a party including the Clifford Morrisons and the Morse family. An English explorer, Mr. Barton, had offered to lead them over a northern route into upper Burma. This trail went over part of the great Himalayas, a route rarely traversed by foreigners and never by white women or children. This turned out to be an incredible journey, taking seventy-seven days. It was remarkable that in spite of un-believable hardships the entire party, including children, finally made it through safely to the British Fort Hertz.

While waiting in Wei-hsi, Vicky and I sent many of our boxes with precious belongings to the Lisu, to bury somewhere for safe-keeping while we were away.

"When will you come back?" asked David Ho anxiously.

"Just as soon as I can," I assured him, shaking his hand warmly. "I shall take a short furlough just long enough to get married to Miss Ada, then we shall return together."

Then taking leave, we waved good-bye to the faithful national couple who were now responsible for keeping the gospel fires burning while the missionaries were away.

One compensation for these events was that Ada and I could get married sooner. Instead of waiting until she returned from her furlough, I would meet her in America after visiting my family in England. We would then be married in her home church in Lancaster, Pennsylvania.

It was a joyful reunion with my parents and relatives who had supported me with their prayers. New happiness had come to Vicky, who had met and married a young preacher, Harry Fisher. He had received a call to China when he was filled with the Holy Spirit. The New Zealand dentist who had been sending support for Vicky had died suddenly, so I felt led to have my Tibetan Border Mission support transferred to her. I was hoping to become affiliated with Ada's American missions board. My parents were not too enthusiastic about this, but their having met and fallen in love with my bride-to-be made this change more acceptable to them.

Sad at leaving my family, but eager to see Ada again, I set sail for the United States. The rough seas made me all the more happy to finally see the skyline of New York City. As we pulled into the dock I scanned the crowds on the pier, searching for a beloved face. Then my impatience spawned a bright, though unconventional idea. Taking a deep breath and cupping my hands, I shouted as loudly as I could, in Chinese: "Pao Mu-sze! Wei-hsi ke jen tsai pa?" ("Bolton here! Anyone there from Wei-hsi?") I waited breathlessly. In a few seconds, between the musical numbers of the ship's band and above the noise of the crowd, I heard the answering call: "Wei-hsi ke jen, tsai le!" ("Wei-hsi people are here!") Mary's voice, stronger than Ada's, had penetrated the noise; it gave me direction. I lost no time getting to them.

Upon looking into Ada's face, however, I was overcome with shyness. But she gave me a welcoming smile, and we were in each other's arms, oblivious to anything else.

Then, with a warm greeting to Mary, I said, "I heard you above all that noise!"

"*My* voice can reach anywhere," she laughed.

After a few days in New York City, our friend Allan Swift approached me. "Do you need a car for your travels in America?"

"I sure do," I answered.

"Well, I know of one you can get for $100," he said. Taking me outside he showed me a Model T Ford. One look was enough.

"I'll take it!" I said. We called it Lizzie.

As I drove Ada and Mary toward Lancaster I couldn't help observing, "What luxury compared to riding a mule!"

"Not as good as Jerry," Mary defended. In a way she was right. Jerry could keep us from getting lost. Lizzie couldn't.

At last we pulled up to the front door of a white farmhouse in Paradise. Ada's mother gave us a very warm welcome, trying to cover up her slight shock at seeing the "worldly" Englishman with bow tie and mustache that her daughter was going to marry. She soon took me into her heart.

We were married on April 7, 1928, in the Lancaster church by the pastor, Rev. Vernon Gortner. A reception was given in the home of my brother-in-law Omar Buchwalter and his wife, Ada.

An unusual aspect of the wedding was its broadcast over the local radio station. Friends for twenty miles around heard our ceremony on their radios. Gifts of money were sent in by many people who had known the Buchwalter family.

All too soon for Ada's mother, the time came for us to leave. As I stooped to kiss the gallant little white-haired lady, she said, "You'll take care of my baby, won't you?"

"I promise with all my heart," I reassured her. As we drove away, Ada kept her tear-blurred gaze on the small, familiar figure in black until she was hidden from view. That was to be her last look at her mother.

Our Model T proved to be a faithful companion as we traveled around the Eastern States, spending a couple of days at Niagara Falls for our honeymoon, visiting churches, and doing some sightseeing along the way. We enjoyed the cherry blossoms at Washington, D.C.

When we arrived at the missions headquarters of the General Council of the Assemblies of God in Springfield, Missouri, I was very apprehensive about appearing before the Foreign Missions Committee.

"Don't worry," Ada reassured me. "They are always glad when we single ladies find a missionary husband. It relieves some of the responsibility they feel for us," she added with a chuckle.

I grew to appreciate that merry little chuckle. It helped us through many difficult situations.

I found it a joy to be accepted by the Fellowship in Springfield and to be given missionary appointment. Stanley Frodsham, a friend of our family from England, and his wife Alice warmly welcomed us.

We then started out for the West Coast in our valiant Model T along Highway 66. Crossing the desert was an experience. We drove at night to keep the tires from melting in the heat. Even at that I had to change tires quite often. Filling stations were literally few and far between. By this time Ada was expecting our first child.

After many days of travel we reached California. We spoke at the district camp meetings, and through contacts made there, we were able to raise the remaining amount of pledged support.

At one point north of Los Angeles, as we drove toward Ventura, the uphill grade became quite steep. Because the fuel pump was not yet part of the Model T engine, the carburetor was gravity fed. So even though the gasoline tank at the back of the car was half full, it may as well have been empty. And we were miles from a filling station.

"If this were Jerry we could dismount and hold his tail while he pulled us up," said Ada.

That gave me an idea. I turned the Model T around. Putting the engine in reverse, I began to back up the hill. It worked! This brought the gasoline forward, taking us backward—all the way up the hill.

In Oakland, we met a Mr. Berry, who was in charge of the Home of Peace, a rest home for missionaries. He had heard that I needed a DC generator for our mission station in China. Taking me to San Francisco, he purchased not only the generator, but also all the wiring, bulbs, and miscellaneous equipment I would need to generate electricity. God had provided from an unexpected source! All

I would need when I got back to China was some farmer's permission to use his waterwheel.

Finally, after selling our faithful Model T that had taken us over ten thousand miles, we completed preparations, took leave of friends and relatives, and set our course once more for China.

On board our freighter was a new fellow missionary, Jarmila Kucera. Of Czechoslovakian origin, she was only five feet tall, but all five feet were full of faith, courage, and the Holy Spirit. We were glad to learn that she, too, felt a call to Yunnan Province and would be working in the same area we were.

After six weeks of monotonous sailing, I said to Ada, "I wish something would happen around here. It's so dull!"

I got my wish—but wished I hadn't! We sailed into a typhoon that tossed our ship about like a cork. The mast broke and the cargo shifted back and forth, causing the ship to list badly. All of the passengers were terribly seasick. For two long days Ada and I endured, water seeping into our cabin all the while. How we prayed!

At last the ship limped into Yokohama, Japan, and with gratitude we set foot on solid ground. After visiting several missionaries and churches in Japan, we sailed for Hong Kong where I had an opportunity to speak at the Boat Mission. Located in the Aberdeen harbor area, the Boat Mission was trying to reach with the gospel the half million people who spent their entire lives housed in boats.

Following a rough three-day voyage on a French steamer, accompanied by a cargo of pigs, we arrived in Haiphong. There we took the long French-Indo China train ride to Kunming where we would await the birth of our child, which I was anticipating with joy and a little anxiety.

The Anglican hospital, where we planned for our baby to be born, was located just outside the city gate, which was closed at night. As the time drew near we decided Ada should go each night to the hospital to sleep, in case she went into labor during the night. I rigged up a bell so she could rouse the Chinese nurses, notorious for the soundness of their sleep while on night duty. In February 1929, our son Robert was born. Chinese culture came to the forefront as the Chinese nurses fussed over this rather scrawny boy baby, exclaiming at this "beauty," while a truly beautiful girl baby of other missionaries was virtually ignored.

Before we left on the ever-dangerous trip north to Wei-hsi, I asked Pastor Albert Wood, an English Pentecostal missionary, to dedicate our infant. During the little ceremony held in a Chinese church, I bowed my head and silently gave thanks to God for my new wife and son.

When the baby was six weeks old we started our journey. Ada rode in a *hua-kan* while holding the baby in a basket in her arms. Because bandit activity was still so prevalent, we had to travel with a soldier escort in a group of more than a hundred people. This made finding a place to sleep at night difficult. We coped with mosquitoes, bugs, bees, crowded quarters, and the problem of milk for the baby. We put a hot water bottle in his basket when we climbed over the snowy mountains. Despite all the hardships, the baby slept well, like the true missionary he was destined to be.

As we approached Wei-hsi, our hearts beat faster. It had been two years since we had been forced to leave. Very little news had filtered through. What would we find now?

At the final descent from Li-ti-p'ing we saw them. Coming to meet us was a great company of Lisu and Chinese Christians, led by Pastor Ho and his wife Ruth. God had not only kept them true, but had also added to their number. What a welcome we were given, and how we rejoiced to see them!

As we settled in, our first problem was obtaining milk for the baby. The answer came when the French Catholic priest who now resided in the only other mission in town sold us a cow. When I first saw the animal—half yak, half cow, one ear missing—I wondered. But a Tibetan woman who had come to help us, Chiang Ta-ma, knew how to handle the beast. Putting salt on her own head, she busied herself with milking while the animal occupied itself with licking.

One of the tasks I tackled was setting up the DC generator I had brought. One of the Christians, Teng Tze-fu, had a mill with two waterwheel units a short distance from town. He agreed to let me install the generator in a room next to one waterwheel. I engaged a carpenter to make a system of shafts and bearings and large and small wooden wheels; on these I put belts to increase speed at the generator. When all was prepared, Shui-an, Teng's son, opened the sluice gate to permit water to flow over the waterwheel. Wheels turned, belts flew, and the generator's armature revolved faster and faster. A bulb in a socket I had hung from a rafter began to burn dimly, then grew brighter. Mr. Teng's eyes almost popped out of their sockets.

"Magic light made from water!" he exclaimed in amazement. Bright lights at his mill and home rewarded him for his kindness to me.

To bring the power lines to our mission compound meant installing wires across rice paddies and a graveyard. The local inhabitants feared these wires would "eat up the water" and disturb the spirits of the departed. They were ready to tear down the wires. I finally persuaded them to allow a trial period. When they saw no harm came of it they allowed the wire and poles to remain intact.

The installation of electricity in our compound brought two distinct blessings: the great convenience of lights, radio, power tools, and an electric iron, and the opportunity to witness. As word got around, people would walk for several days just to see the miracle of "lights made out of water." This was a ready-made audience to hear about Christ: the Water of Life, the Light of the World.

In March 1930, a new baby came to our household, this time a daughter. Jarmila Kucera, our small Czech friend from our return voyage, had come to join us. She and I were the "midwives." We almost lost the baby; the umbilical cord was wrapped around her neck. I prayed desperately that God would spare her, and at that moment life pulsated into her tiny body. We named her Elsie. She soon began to thrive on the rich cow's milk we had for her.

Another blessing was Chiang Ta-ma, a devoted helper—especially with the children, who returned her affection. With her help and the motherly care of "Aunty Jean," as we called Jarmila, Ada soon felt free to travel with me to the mountains. I had been to some of the villages, but we were anxious to see how the Lisu in other villages were faring after our long absence.

We were elated to find them faithfully attending church, singing their Lisu hymns, and studying their Gospel portions and catechisms. They gave us an exuberant welcome. At many places they prepared a feast of welcome: a sheep or goat would be slaughtered, long tables of rough boards set up, and bowls of steaming rice, vegetables, and meat set before us.

"We are so happy that you two have joined together and have come to bless us with your presence" was their affirming consensus.

In each village we dedicated babies, baptized new converts, and taught God's Word. Some places had new chapels to be dedicated. To see the happiness on these Lisu faces was worth all the difficult travel and uncomfortable quarters—sleeping on boards at night in drafty, smoky one-room huts. These Lisu Christians were our "children in the Lord" and we rejoiced in each one.

During the Easter and Christmas seasons we held large conventions at Wei-hsi, using a big tent we had brought with us and erected in the mission compound yard. Surveying the people who came, we noted Lisu, Tibetans, Chinese, and others of mixed blood—all worshiping together in wonderful harmony. Was this not another miracle?

The work among the Lisu people began to spread. We ordered hundreds of Lisu Gospels and hymnbooks. These were printed in Kunming and brought to us by mule caravan. Other missionaries had come to minister among the Lisu. The Russell Morses and Isobel Maxey, Christian Church missionaries, had opened a work among the Lisu to the north of us. The Clifford Morrisons, Assemblies of God missionaries like us, had opened a mission at Shang-pa, five days away in the Salween River area.

We also had the joy of welcoming back my sister Vicky and her husband, Harry Fisher, supported by the Tibetan Border Mission. After prayer they decided to open a mission at Lan-p'ing among the Chinese, Nosu, and Minchia people. This was an area Ada, Alfred, and Mary had evangelized years before and claimed for God. We praised the Lord that now a definite, long-term work would be established there.

We found the work among the Chinese in Wei-hsi and the Lisu in the mountains so rewarding that another year passed virtually unnoticed.

Our pattern of activity was broken by a trip to the dentist—in

Hanoi, more than six hundred miles away. There Ada could get a set of false teeth. I had already extracted quite a few of the problem teeth with dental forceps and no anesthetic. She had endured the pain as bravely as she had endured childbirth, with a silent prayer to heaven for strength and fortitude.

We set out on our journey, Ada and I on horseback and the two small children seated back to back in a specially devised *hua-kan* carried by coolies. At one time the nimble-footed coolies got far ahead of us. We did not catch up until the next village—to the distress of our children. Surrounded by a curious crowd, and frightened by all the strange faces, upon seeing us, the children called, "Mommy! Daddy!" with obvious relief.

While at Hanoi, Elsie and Bob contracted chicken pox, which delayed our return trip. But finally we set off with a fresh supply of sugar, tea, and coffee, and Ada's new set of teeth!

One snowy morning in March 1932 we were blessed with another daughter, Irene. Mary Lewer was now back from furlough and she and Chiang Ta-ma helped at the birth. The baby thrived and grew rapidly.

One day a letter arrived from Ada's brother, Omar Buchwalter, with the sad news that Mother Buchwalter had passed away. "She seemed to linger until she heard the new baby had arrived safely," Omar wrote, "then she slipped quietly into heaven." She never saw Ada's children, but each letter she wrote had been full of faith and encouragement. The "brave ones" are not only those who go overseas.

No doubt it was their grandmother's prayers and later those of others that brought the Lord's protection to our children. One afternoon while Ada and I were resting, Elsie came toddling into the room. "Mommy, Mommy! Monkey eat baby's sweater!" I ran out and found our pet monkey had gotten loose and was sitting on baby Irene in the carriage picking at her sweater. Thank God, the baby was unharmed! Nevertheless, we gave away the monkey.

On another occasion three-year-old Elsie was walking by the hand pump of our well. Suddenly I saw a big snake coiled around the pump! Before I could get to her the snake uncoiled itself and slithered between her feet. Later, when caught and killed, the black reptile measured four feet long.

Even though raising a family in this country had its perils, it was rewarding to know that it strengthened our witness among the people. Unwanted Chinese baby girls were often thrown over the city wall where wolves would come and devour their tiny bodies. By contrast, the people observed our happy family. They were curious about our life-style and took note of how we loved and cared for one another. This was a more potent sermon than any we could preach. So these little ones God had given us were not the least of those who had come to join forces in spreading the wonderful message of the gospel in the Orient.

Ada with her Autoharp

The Boltons with their Model T Ford, 1928

Jubilant Lisu believers being baptized in water by David Ho (Ada Bolton is in the background.)

Lisu Christmas convention

Lisu fellowship at the Wei-hsi mission

Joining forces: *(left to right)* Ruth and David Ho, Ada and Leonard Bolton, Jean and Harvey Wagner

Carrying water: an everyday job for this Lisu woman.

The children (Elsie, Irene, and Bob) imitating the Lisu

15

Evangelists to the Lisu

The "Black Lisu" of the Upper Mekong River territory where we labored were among the poorest of earth's peoples. Yet they had retained a fiercely independent spirit as well as their own cultural identity. The description "black" did not refer to color but to custom and mode of dress.

Farther south and west in the Salween Canyon area were the "Flowery Lisu" with their more colorful attire. To these Flowery Lisu the CIM pioneer missionary J. O. Fraser first gained an entrance in 1908. Having mastered Mandarin Chinese, he also learned their Lisu dialect and painstakingly devised a phonetic script. Then he translated the New Testament Gospels and a hymnbook into Lisu.

The Black Lisu and the Flowerly Lisu, as well as other subgroups of the Lisu, had a strong clan system and similar religious beliefs. Like the Chinese, they worshiped their ancestors; unlike the Chinese, they did not worship idols. Instead, they were animists; they worshiped spirits said to reside in the trees, in the earth, and in the wind. They believed in guardian spirits of the villages, a lord of heaven, a lightning demon, and spirits of the fields and crops. In their homes they had spirit shelves on which they would place sacrificial food offerings. Malevolent spirits were feared as causing troubles and illnesses. When something adverse occurred the Lisu would hire a sorcerer to try to exorcise the demons thought to be responsible. Along the paths leading into their villages were small altars where they would place food offerings to placate the spirits.

The Lisu were looked down on by many Chinese as "earth people" and were oppressed by the overlords who demanded taxes. In addition, their young men were conscripted into the Chinese army, some of them never to be heard of again.

Theirs was a hard life. But in spite of their privations, laughter came readily to the Lisu; they found pleasure in little things.

God's work among the Lisu is a beautiful picture of the ways of God. First, He prepared them to receive the message through the work of the Holy Spirit. They were expecting men to come with "the Book." Then, with His marvelous timing, He prepared messengers. From various parts of the world He brought them: J. O. Fraser from England, to devise a phonetic script as a vehicle for the message; Mary Buchwalter from America and Alfred Lewer from England; followed soon by Ada Buchwalter and me; then the Clifford Morrisons from Canada, and others—each having his or her special place of ministry.

EVANGELISTS TO THE LISU were not limited to those coming from overseas. In 1921, Alfred wrote Mr. Fraser asking him to send a couple of his flowery Lisu evangelists to help evangelize the Black Lisu around Wei-hsi. He was hoping the dialects would be similar so the Bible portions and songs Fraser had translated could be used. Since Mr. Fraser's burden was broad, he sent two fine evangelists to Wei-hsi. It was a happy day when they discovered that, despite slight differences, the Lisu dialects could be understood by both tribes. This meant the alphabet could be taught among, and their literature used by, the Black Lisu.

These two intrepid lay preachers endured the rigors and hardships of traveling from village to village, evangelizing the people. They assured the villagers that Pastor Lewer would not exploit them but would teach them from "the Book." The sacrificial dedication of these young men away from their own homes, farms, and people resulted in one hundred families being won to the Lord. When Mr. Fraser heard this thrilling report he was overjoyed.

These men had become a bridge, opening the way for Alfred Lewer to follow their witness with teaching and further evangelization. Alfred took David Ho with him to the villages and they established churches and baptized believers. On one trip he and

David baptized two hundred believers, dedicated two new chapels, and enrolled over one hundred inquirers.

AN OUTSTANDING COUPLE, David and Ruth Ho were uniquely suited to evangelizing the people. They could speak five languages between them and despite hardships had proved faithful during the absence of missionaries. They had received a lucrative offer to work somewhere else but had turned it down because it would have meant giving up their testimony.

Their discipleship began in this way: When Alfred and Mary first went as pioneer missionaries to A-teng-tze on the Tibetan border, they were expecting their first baby. Mary prayed that God would send a girl whom she could train to help her. Their cook, Timothy, heard about the need and brought his young sister Ah Hsi-lan to them. She looked quite forlorn, her clothes tattered and ragged. But Mary taught her to cook, wash, iron, and clean house.

Ah Hsi-lan was happy and grateful for all that she was taught. Although she was seventeen years old, she had never been to school. Under Mary's tutorship, she quickly learned to read the Word of God and accepted Christ as her Saviour. When she was baptized she adopted the Bible name of Ruth.

For many years Ruth's mother had sought for peace. She had tried Buddhism, taking her offerings of rice and chicken to the mountain temples and placing bowls of incense before the idols. She had taken a vegetarian vow and memorized the words of the priests as they chanted their prayers. She had even tried the Islamic faith and imitated their prayers and religious ritual. Then she contracted a disease. Knowing she was dying, she called her children to her bedside. "Everything is so dark," she moaned. "It's so dark—but there *must* be light somewhere. Keep looking. Look for Truth!"

Ruth never forgot her mother's words, and she determined to continue her mother's quest. When she was brought to the Lewers by her brother and heard for the first time of Jesus and the Heavenly Father, she knew her quest was ended.

She became a great blessing to the Lewers. They had been suffering extreme hardships at A-teng-tze. No one would sell them anything. Buddhist priests had told people "their money will turn to leaves." But in answer to persistent prayer, God moved on people to come to their door at night with wood, charcoal, potatoes, squash, and turnips. Gratefully Alfred and Mary purchased these supplies. Ruth was there to negotiate for them.

Once Mary became very ill. While Alfred prayed for her day and night, Ruth kept things running until God healed Mary. She stood by the Lewers when all their efforts to reach the Tibetans met with disheartening results.

Alfred and Mary journeyed to Pa-t'ang for the birth of their first baby. The return trip was a nightmarish one. Battling rain, mud, and uncooperative coolies, they lost their way in the mountains. With a small baby in arms this was catastrophic. Only faith in God saw them through. In the midst of all these difficulties, the beautiful conversion of Ruth was a real encouragement to them. When their little son died so tragically, Ruth was the only other woman present to comfort Mary. She became a very special person to the Lewers.

However, Alfred's first contact with David was not so auspicious. After settling in Wei-hsi, Alfred prayed for a reliable young man to assist him on trips, help care for the horses, and do chores. The Klavers at Li-chiang had working with them an evangelist who had heard of Alfred's need. He sent his orphan nephew to be Alfred's helper. The young man, Ho Tsan-dien, came from the Nashi tribe.

At first, it seemed to Alfred that young Ho would not amount to much. He even smoked opium. However, Ho soon proved himself to be teachable and dependable. During one arduous trip in frigid weather, the young man pointed to a large log some distance away and observed, "I think if I could get that big log down the hillside for firewood, we would stay warm all night."

Alfred doubted that he could do it. But to his surprise he later discovered that with great persistence Ho had tugged and pulled the log into the camp. That night they slept by a good fire, protected from wild animals and the cold mountain air.

In a letter home to England Alfred wrote, "If I have love for this young man, and patience, and added patience, I believe something good will come of him."

Alfred patiently educated young Ho, giving him the Word of God as well. The Lord saved him and delivered him from his addiction to opium. After his water baptism Ho took the name of David. He received the baptism in the Holy Spirit and spent hours each night studying God's Word by the light of a small kerosene lantern.

As David developed, Alfred gave him opportunity to testify and preach. David possessed a natural talent for speaking and was becoming a real asset to the ministry.

One day the Lewers suggested to David that Ruth would make him a good wife. He exclaimed, "O praise the Heavenly Father!" But then he told them, "I cannot ask her." According to their customs, a marriage had to be arranged by the parents or guardians, through a middleman.

Alfred lost no time. He made sure Ruth was in agreement. Then, since her father was dead, he contacted Ruth's older brother. To his alarm, Alfred learned that the brother was planning to marry Ruth to a heathen businessman. Only by much prayer and tactful management was the brother finally persuaded to change his mind and permit Ruth to marry David.

It was the first Christian wedding in the town and it made quite an impression. Usually a Chinese bride is unhappy because she becomes a servant to her mother-in-law. But the people commented about Ruth, "The bride looks so happy!"

Then came the traumatic experience of Alfred's drowning. David had been selected by Alfred as one of the party to accompany him to Bhamo to meet me. At the Mekong River, he watched helplessly as his beloved missionary went to his watery grave. Devastated, David fell to his knees beside the river and made a total dedication of his life to the Lord. He prayed, "Oh God, help me to continue the work my pastor has been cut off from doing!" This was a turning point in his life. The Holy Spirit came upon him in power, and David became an untiring preacher and co-worker.

Ruth and David were an invaluable blessing to the work. Often we would hear them praying together for the needs of the people. And the Lisu would flock to their house.

ALTHOUGH ADA THOUGHT OF THE HOS as instrumental in the work among the Lisu, she made her contribution as well.

They made a team as they traveled from village to village. Her

Autoharp playing and their singing would draw a crowd. After Ada spoke, Ruth or David would preach. They would then give out tracts and sell Gospel portions.

At one village called Yin Ping Kai (meaning Salt Well), the people spoke a dialect of the Ming-chia tribe. Ada, David, and Ruth sang and spoke in Mandarin Chinese, which a few of the villagers could understand. The people stopped their marketing, gathered around, and listened with great interest. As Ruth gave the gospel message they were most attentive.

When the service was over, a man came to them and said in Mandarin, "Oh! You speak wonderful Ming-chia!"

"I don't understand a word of it," Ruth exclaimed. She turned to Ada in puzzlement. Ada, too, was astounded. She had spoken in Mandarin. Had God performed a miracle and let it enter the ears of those people in their own language?

At Wa Ti, a Lisu village, quite a few families accepted the Lord. Then, a gentle old man begged them to come to his village of T'o Ti. They consented and were accompanied by twelve men from Wa Ti. The old man's wife came to meet them, bringing tea and some food. Ruth and Ada were invited to one house after another to pray for the sick and talk about the Lord. God wonderfully touched sick bodies and opened the minds and hearts of the poor villagers to the Lord.

Going to the village of Ne Bu Lu was another matter. It took a lot of courage, for it had the reputation of being a robber stronghold. The headman himself was a bandit. The boldness of Ada and Ruth came from the prayer that had been made for the village. Putting up their song sheets and Bible pictures in the village market, they started to teach the gospel. When the headman came and sat right in front, however, they grew uncomfortable. He watched and listened intently, at times nodding his head. They were not sure what he was thinking or what he intended to do.

When they concluded, he stood up. Looking over the crowd of villagers gathered around, he commanded them all to stand. Then he faced Ada and Ruth. "This is wonderful truth you are telling us. Never have I heard of a God who loves us! Your story touches my heartstrings. This Yeh-su [Jesus] who died for us—we should serve

Him as our Leader. We must put away our belief in other spirits and follow Him."

Instructing the villagers to follow suit, he raised his hand toward God in surrender to Him. Soon the sound of weeping could be heard as people, falling to the ground under conviction, confessed their sins to God. On that occasion about fifty families at once surrendered their lives to Jesus. That evening around a large crackling campfire, the two women again expounded the gospel message. And again the villagers responded in prayer, confession of sins, and repentance.

Before they left, Ruth suggested to the headman, "Perhaps some of your men can come back with us to Wei-hsi for more teaching." He and others heartily agreed. Consequently, two men returned with them for training to become elders in the new church that was formed. Later a chapel would be built from the trees of the former spirit grove. Ninety percent of the village genuinely turned to Christ and the new church was established with two hundred fifty Christians. The bandit chief himself was delivered from opium smoking and became a very kind and gracious man.

One day a Lisu man came into our mission compound visibly trembling. Some Chinese antagonists had told him, "If you go in there they'll kill you! They'll make medicine out of your eyes!"

He had stayed outside the gate of the compound all day, listening for any unusual sounds. But all he heard was happy talking and singing. Finally he gathered courage to venture in.

"I heard that you have a Book," he said hesitantly. That was all David needed to hear. Long into the night he expounded the Word of God to the man, Mei P'a. "If only our village could have the gospel!" Mei P'a pleaded. So a man who had been studying with David was sent with him.

A few weeks later when Ada went to the village with David many had already accepted Christ. She spent a few days there teaching them more of the Word of God. Then Mei P'a came to her with a petition. "The villagers of Kon Go just across the river are begging to hear this gospel. Won't you please come with me and tell them?"

Across the river! thought Ada. She lay awake that night in the little log cabin, watching the smoke from the dying fire as it drifted out through the cracks, listening to the river as it roared within its banks (though it was yet a good distance away). Her body produced its own sensations: the pounding heart within her chest, the pulsating blood in her ears. She could not quiet herself, so she prayed.

Then the Lord spoke. "You promised to go wherever I would send you," He reminded her. "Don't you believe I can take care of you?"

"Yes, Lord," she bowed in answer. "I do believe. Please pour Your peace into my heart."

The next morning Lisu carriers hoisted her bedding and other goods onto their backs. David carried the Scripture portions and hymn sheets. All too soon for Ada they came to the great Mekong's banks. She felt small and alone, and the dugouts carved from tree trunks seemed more risky than ever. The other side of the river looked so far away.

Then Ada thought of how far the Lord Jesus had come to save her, and He was with her still. Taking the boatman's hand, she stepped into the little craft. More uncertain than Ada was her horse, looking deeply insulted at being held firmly at one end by the tail and at the other end by the jaw to keep him from upsetting the boat. Although she knew it was coming, the grab of the current caught her breath away as the boatman pushed off. She welcomed the opposite shore with relief.

News had already reached the village, and a delegation had come to escort the missionary party up the trail to where about a hundred villagers had gathered. They were eager to hear the story of Jesus. After the message, they expressed their desire to become believers; then they led the way from hut to hut as they stripped off all the artifacts of their spirit worship: red papers, incense sticks, and spirit shelves. It all went up in smoke in a big bonfire in the center of the village. Many faces were bathed in tears of repentance as the people lifted their voices in worship and commitment. Their response more than compensated Ada for her trial in crossing the Mekong.

Later, when David and I went to Kon Go we baptized over one hundred converts!

David Ho, his wife Ruth, and their sons (John, their oldest, is in the middle.)

A Lisu believer—"laughter came readily"

16
Lisu Leaders

"What did you say?" croaked the old woman, struggling to sit up on the sleeping mat. The maze of wrinkles on her face deepened as she strained to see us.

"Jesus loves you!"

"Huh? Nobody wants *me!* I have lived beyond my usefulness. I cannot work in the fields, bear children, or grind the corn. I have been waiting long for death to come and take me. But even death doesn't want me!"

Ruth and Ada then told her about the Saviour who had died for her sins, conquered death by coming back from the dead, and offered life forever with Him in heaven.

"You mean, even to a *woman?*" asked the daughter of the old woman in amazement. "Even to *us,* who are of no more worth than cows?"

"Absolutely! To *all* who believe. The Book says so. Jesus counted us women worthy enough to die for. He gives us this life now which will continue after our bodies die."

The news that the gospel included women was received with joyful thankfulness by the Lisu women; they in turn brought great blessing to God's work. God used them, as well as the men, to extend His church.

At a village one day, Ada felt impressed to use a Bible story picture of Hannah, telling how in answer to Hannah's prayer God gave her a son, Samuel. Afterwards, Ada was put on the spot. A young woman named La Du Ma rushed to her and, kneeling down, said urgently, "Please pray for me right now! Pray that God will give *me* a son." Ada prayed, believing.

The following year La Du Ma's husband came to Wei-hsi. "The Lord has answered your prayer!" he beamed, presenting us with a

live chicken he had tucked in his shirt. "My wife gave birth to a
fine son. We are naming him Sa Ma Li [Samuel]. Will you please
come for the dedication of the baby and share a feast of thanks?"

We learned that La Du Ma was the daughter of Ao Ma, an outstanding Lisu leader. At the feast, Ao Ma told us how desperate the
need had been. Since La Du Ma had not borne any children, the
husband's heathen father had been insisting that, according to clan
obligation, his son take another wife to produce the needed heir.
God's timely answer had saved them from this! Later, God blessed
them with another son, Isaac, who grew to be a leader in the church.
T'a Ma, the lovely daughter who followed, also had a place in God's
plan.

AO MA WAS IN HER FIFTIES when she first walked into Wei-hsi.
She wanted to hear about "the book with good news in it." She
listened hungrily to the preaching, then exchanged some eggs for
a gospel booklet.

"Won't you please read it to me?" she begged. Ruth Ho sat with
her long into the night; the new day found Ao Ma praising and
thanking God for the light that had dawned in her heart.

"What can I do for Jesus?" she asked Ruth.

"Get rid of the corn pipe you have stuck in your belt," Ruth
instructed. "Our bodies are temples of the Holy Spirit so we must
not defile them by smoking."

"I no longer wanted it, anyhow," Ao Ma said, throwing her pipe
into the fire. "Now what can I do?"

"Go sell your silver tribal earrings and ornaments, and give the
money to God," Ruth suggested.

Ao Ma came back some time later. "I have done what you told
me," she said. "Now what else can I do for the Lord Jesus?"

"Give yourself," was the answer. "Learn to read the Book, then
go to your village and tell your people about Jesus."

Ao Ma obeyed. She worked diligently day after day to master the
phonetic script of the Lisu language and to learn to read the Bible.
After seeking the Lord in prayer and praise, she was gloriously
baptized in the Holy Spirit. The Spirit's power helped her to grasp
truth.

Then one day she announced, "Now I am ready to go."

On the trail up the mountain she met two men leading a sheep, "to give to the Buddhist priest," one of them told her.

"My six-month-old baby is sick," explained the other sadly. "I am taking this, my last sheep, as a sacrifice, hoping to appease the wrath of the spirits. All my children have died as babies. I want so much to keep this last one."

"The priest cannot save your baby!" declared Ao Ma boldly. "I know—no priest has been able to help me. But I know of a Great One in heaven who does hear and answer prayer. He can heal your baby. Would you like me to come and pray for him?"

The father hesitated, but as Ao Ma continued to talk about Jesus, the Saviour of both soul and body, he consented. "We will see if what you say is the truth. We will test your God and see if He can save my baby. Come with us."

Ao Ma trudged over two mountain ranges with the men. Finally they arrived at Hsi Lan, a village of no more than a dozen small wooden shanties clinging to the steep mountainside.

Upon entering the dark squalid hut, Ao Ma found the infant emaciated and covered with eczema. The father prepared to kill his sheep as a sacrifice.

"No need to do that!" Ao Ma declared. "Just get rid of your demon altar and sacred sticks, and turn from worshiping spirits to worshiping the true, living God."

She washed the baby, then tenderly rubbed the tiny body with oil. Lifting her eyes to heaven she prayed, "Lord God, heal this baby and save the people in this village."

Ao Ma remained at Hsi Lan a number of days watching the sores dry up. The baby miraculously recovered. In the marketplace she declared that Jesus is the only Saviour. Not only the baby's father, but also the village chief believed, followed by most of the villagers. Night after night Ao Ma taught them from the Book and they learned hymns from the songbook. Presently she told them, "I must go on to other villages. If you would like a teacher and a Book for yourselves you must send someone to the mission at Wei-hsi." This they readily did. A Lisu worker was then sent to teach their people.

Later, when David and I traveled to Hsi Lan, a grass-roofed

chapel had been built by the believers and fifty people were ready for water baptism.

Ao Ma returned to her village of La Pa Ti and cleaned out her own hut, ridding it of the spirit shelf. Some of the villagers scoffed at her message, but she persisted in her witness. Eventually about thirty people, half of the village, became believers. It was here that David spent several months learning the Lisu dialect from Ao Ma.

Ao Ma continued her pilgrimage from village to village. Over the rough mountain trails she climbed, often weary and footsore, but always with a prayer in her heart and a song on her lips. God was working through her to bring salvation and healing to her people.

She was not always welcomed. One chief resented her influence and forbade his people to receive her. As she approached his village one day, he set his fierce wolf-dog on her. Baring its teeth in a snarl, it leaped up and bit a piece out of Ao Ma's cheek. Quickly, she called on the Lord. Then in the name of Jesus, she rebuked the inevitable infection from spreading in her body. Covering the bleeding wound with her hand, she walked into the village. But all doors were closed to her. Sadly she turned and went on to a neighboring village.

Later at Wei-hsi she told how the Lord had healed her, and showed us how the wound had miraculously closed, leaving only a small scar as a testimony of God's deliverance.

One day near the entrance to a remote village, Ao Ma came across a poor outcast leper woman cowering beside the trail. Her body was covered with putrefying sores. Coming closer Ao Ma saw maggots eating into the live tissues of the leper's body. Moved with compassion, she spoke soothingly to the frightened woman. Then she plucked the maggots away and washed her sores, all the while speaking of the love of Jesus. After applying oil to the now bleeding wounds, she laid her hands on the woman's shoulders and prayed fervently, under a powerful anointing of the Holy Spirit. Then she lifted the woman to her feet and accompanied her back to her home, a hut on a high ledge away from the village.

About a week later while partaking of Communion, Ao Ma felt led to take some of the bread and fruit juice up to the leper's hut to share Communion with her. She found the woman much improved. As the leper received the elements of Communion, divine power flowed into her body, completely healing her leprosy and enabling her to walk upright. The former leper and Ao Ma broke into rejoicing. This marvelous deliverance meant the outcast could rejoin her village.

Several years went by. Then a wave of persecution swept over the Lisu churches during a political upheaval. Ao Ma was at her house beside the La Pa Ti church when runners came with the word that bandits were on their way to attack. The villagers fled with what valuables they could take with them. Ao Ma's husband called to her to follow.

"No, I will not run away," she declared. "The bandits must not burn down the house of God." She put a large pot of water on the fire and waited.

Soon the stillness was rent with wild cries as the bandits stormed into the village. Suddenly they stopped dead and stared at the old woman sitting serenely in her doorway.

Politely she said to the leader and his men, "Would you like some tea?" Baffled, they accepted the tea and drank it.

Then they asked, "Why haven't you run away like the rest?"

"Because I'm a Christian believer and I don't want you to burn our church."

The rest of the village was plundered and burned, but Ao Ma, her house, and the church were left unharmed.

Years later the time came when Ao Ma could no longer travel. She knew her Lord would soon take her home. But she desired one thing above all else before she died. One by one, eight of her children had come to the Lord. But her eldest son had left home at an early age. Rumors had drifted back that he was smoking opium. But Ao Ma had not heard from him in a long time. With what little strength she had left she prostrated herself before God and prayed for her son's conversion. "I know God will answer my prayer before I die," she declared.

Soon she became bedfast. One evening it became evident the end was at hand. Her family gathered around her. Suddenly she raised herself up on one arm.

"What is it?" they asked. "Do you want something to eat?"

"No."

"Do you want something to drink?"

"No." She seemed to be just waiting.

The next moment there was the sound of running, and in came a bleary-eyed man with the telltale yellow tint of an opium smoker.

"Mother!" he cried. "Something inside me made me come home. I want to worship the same God you worship!"

At the sound of his voice Ao Ma lay back, a satisfied, peaceful expression on her face. As her spirit took leave of her body, the last member of her earthly family was born into the kingdom of God.

WE HAD COMPLETED PREPARATIONS for a Bible teaching session when I noticed a young man with his arm in a sling standing shyly in the background.

"My name is Ah Tsu," he said, answering my questions. "I would like to learn more about Yeh-su [Jesus]."

Orphaned at birth, Ah Tsu had been raised by a neighbor—who resented the task because she had eight children of her own. He had worked hard for his keep. One afternoon as he returned from herding the goats, he noticed a crowd in a village clearing gathered around a Lisu woman with an open book in her hand.

"She spoke about strange things such as I had never heard before," Ah Tsu said. "She told of a God who loves and of His Son Yeh-su who died for our sins and who listens when we pray to Him. I could not stay longer, for I had to gather wood and get home soon or my 'aunt' would beat me. But I thought often of the woman's words.

"Time went by. One day when the sun hung low I was chopping down a tree when it suddenly crashed to the ground, pinning my arm under a heavy branch. No one heard my cries for help. Darkness was coming fast. The distant howling of hungry wolves made me realize the horror of my plight. Then I remembered Yeh-su. Would He hear? Could He help me? I prayed desperately—and waited.

"All at once there was a loud crack of thunder. A strong gust of wind swept up the valley and whirled around me. It caught the great branches of the tree, rolling it over. I was free! I forgot the pain in my crushed arm and praised Yeh-su! I now believed in Him. After this I would not worship spirits at the spirit shrine. My aunt was very angry and turned me out of the house. Then I heard about this school where I could learn about Yeh-su from the Book."

Ah Tsu was an apt student. He learned the Lisu phonetic script quickly and drank in the Bible teaching. When he was baptized, he took the name Jonah. As he sought God, he received the baptism in the Holy Spirit. It would have been easier for him to remain in the Wei-hsi area, but he felt the call of God to preach the gospel among the Lisu.

As he neared the village of Horse Thief Flat he met a woman whose face stirred his memory. When she spoke he knew she was the woman with the open Book he had heard years before! It was Ao Ma, "the Bible woman." Happily he told her his story.

"You must come to my house so we can talk more about the things of God," she said.

In the doorway of the humble home stood a young maiden with bright eyes and raven hair. Jonah was smitten. *Who was she?* He thought, *What a wonderful wife she would make for any person!*

"T'a Ma, run quickly and get some tea and cakes. We have a guest with us today."

They talked long into the night. Eagerly, Jonah listened to the wisdom of the Bible woman. The Word was illumined and his heart burned anew with the message of truth.

Ao Ma pointed to her scarred and callused feet. "These feet have trod many miles to spread the good news. They are getting old and tired. You are young and strong. You must carry on the work until every village resounds with the songs of Zion." She pointed to the scar on her cheek. "Do not be afraid of persecution," she said. "The Lord within you will help you to triumph over the enemy."

When Jonah left, he went on his way inspired.

Later, on returning to the mission at Wei-hsi, he brought thrilling reports of all that God had been doing.

One day, I broached a subject David and I had discussed. "There is a matter I want to talk to you about," I said to Jonah. "It concerns your future."

He looked a little alarmed. I continued, "Ao Ma has been here to talk about the possibility of a marriage to her granddaughter, T'a Ma."

Jonah was studying his feet.

"What would you think about such an arrangement, Jonah? If you are willing, we can arrange it for you."

Jonah shuffled his feet, then blurted out, "I am willing!" His excitement revealed that he had fallen in love with T'a Ma.

It was the first Christian wedding in T'a Ma's village. All the people turned out to see the "drinking of wine" ceremony (the Lisu term for a marriage) that had no drinking of wine! Instead of the noisy carousing and dancing all night, with the bridal couple hardly featured at all, they watched this bride and groom make promises to each other before God. The feast was a joyful time with no miserable aftereffects the next day. Something could be said for this kind of wedding!

Jonah and T'a Ma consecrated their lives afresh to the Lord as they went back to Jonah's village to live.

Not long after their first baby was born, a great epidemic raged through the area. A message was sent to T'a Ma's mother, La Du Ma, to come and help her sick daughter and baby. The brave Lisu woman drove her sheep through rugged country over high mountains and across a river to her daughter's home. She nursed T'a Ma and the baby until they recovered, but she herself went to be with the Lord.

Jonah came to see us later and said, "Now I know the difference between someone who dies without God and one who does not. My mother-in-law died in our home with such peace! Her countenance was beautiful, and we were not afraid to touch her as we laid her tenderly in a coffin. We knew she was 'present with the Lord'[1] and one day we will see her again. We had a Christian funeral for her."

What a contrast to the terror of death among the unbelieving Lisu: drums beating for days to scare away evil spirits, loud weeping and wailing to vent the despair.

WHEN CH'I TZU MEI P'A CAME FROM NE BU LU to the mission for teaching, he was poor and uneducated, having barely enough clothes to cover his body. He did not show the usual curiosity about the mission house and the manner of living of the missionaries. He wanted only to learn the answers to questions he had been pondering: What were the signs of the Lord's coming? How was prophecy being fulfilled? What was God doing in other places? He absorbed all the teaching he could. When he later returned to Ne Bu Lu he became a loved and respected elder. But at times he had barely enough to eat.

One day he asked a Chinese acquaintance to lend him money for food. "I'll pay you back soon, when the corn is harvested," he promised.

But the man, antagonistic toward Christians, taunted him, "Why don't you ask your God for food?"

"Yes," replied Ch'i, "you're right. I'll do just that!" He returned home to pray.

The following day he went to inspect some traps he had set in the mountains. To his joy they were full. Their pelts meant money—enough to buy the food he so sorely needed. He also caught fish when others fishing nearby were unsuccessful. God had answered his prayer.

Ch'i Tzu Mei P'a lived mostly on wild honey and fish. I repeatedly offered him some of my clothes but he preferred his sheepskin.

Before he was saved, Ch'i had been an idol maker. God delivered him from the habits of taking opium and gambling, and Ch'i refused to make idols any longer. One day he received orders from the Chinese magistrate to come and repair some idols in a temple in the Wei-hsi area.

"I cannot do it," he declared to the messenger, "for I am now serving the true and living God." He sent word back admonishing the wicked official to turn from his sinful ways or God would punish him.

It was a time of political unrest. However, we held our Christmas convention as usual, putting up a large tent in the mission compound. The magistrate sent orders for us to disband, saying the Lisu were "causing trouble."

After consulting with David, I went to the official and assured him the Christian Lisu were peaceful and law-abiding: They no longer got drunk, smoked opium, or gambled. Begrudgingly, he permitted us to continue our convention—under the watchful eye of soldiers.

I felt a bit uneasy, so after the convention I encouraged David to slip out secretly through a hole in the mud wall and stay with a Lisu believer in another village for a while. I later learned a $200 reward was being offered for killing David!

Then news came to us that Ch'i Tzu Mei P'a had been captured, whipped, and put in the city jail, an indescribably filthy place where rats and vermin were rampant. No food was given to the prisoners; relatives or friends had to bring it to them. I went to the jail with food and clothes, expecting to see a torn and bleeding man lying on the ground.

To my surprise I heard singing. When the jailor unlocked the door, there was Ch'i chained closely to the wall with his hymnbook in his hands, teaching the other prisoners to sing! His clothes were bloodstained and grimy, his swarthy face streaked with dried blood.

When he saw me his face beamed, "Give the food to the other prisoners," he said. "They need it more than I do."

I carefully removed his jacket to treat his wounds. He grimaced and I shuddered. After whipping him the soldiers had rubbed salt into the lacerations. Yet he could sing! He told me that after his torture Someone in white had come to him and touched his back and eased the pain. As I administered ointment to the wounds he further told me how the other prisoners had at first jeered and cursed him while he witnessed to them about Christ.

One particularly rough, hardened character named Lu had reviled him with the most abusive language. Nevertheless, Ch'i continued to tell him that Jesus loved him enough to die for him.

"How can a dead person help me?" Lu muttered.

"But He is not dead now! He rose from the dead and is now in heaven. He will come into our hearts with His everlasting life if we invite Him in. See, it's all written in the Book."

Suddenly Lu showed interest. "My old father used to talk of a Book that someone would bring us someday."

That was the turning point. Gradually his resistance broke down, until in the end he accepted the salvation offered in the Book. Love had won him.

I petitioned the magistrate for Ch'i's release, but to no avail. We continued to bring food, which Ch'i secretly shared with the others, and we continued to pray. Ch'i had been in prison for ten days when we heard the prisoners were to be taken out and shot. Our prayers became even more fervent.

That night we heard a loud knocking at the mission chapel door. When someone opened it, there stood Ch'i Tzu Mei P'a, pale and emaciated, but smiling! I saw something in his face I had not seen before. He had been with the Lord Jesus in suffering and had come out victorious.

Why was he freed? The magistrate had become very ill. One of his soldiers told him, "You will die if you don't let that preacher out of jail!"

Later we heard the other prisoners had been executed.

But those who had accepted Christ went before the firing squad with peace in their hearts and a smile on their faces.

The magistrate was eventually summoned to the provincial capital of Kunming. While traveling, he was captured by bandits and never heard of again.

The hardships and persecution the believers endured served only to refine and strengthen them. God was building up His Church by His Spirit through the choice leaders He was raising up.

---

[1]2 Corinthians 5:8

Ao-ma, "the Bible Woman"

Ch'i Tzu Mei P'a,
"After his torture
Someone in white
. . . touched his back
and eased the pain."

Jonah, Lisu evangelist, with his wife T'a
Ma and baby boy (Their marriage
 represented "the first Christian wedding in
T'a Ma's village.")

17

"The Lord Working With Them"[1]

That God delights to respond to childlike faith was beautifully portrayed in the lives of the Lisu. In simple faith they took God at His word and he blessed them.

Their leaders periodically received Bible teaching from the missionaries. Then, from a simple catechism they instructed their people.

The leaders taught the people that to receive salvation they must truly repent. They must turn from spirit worship, drunken reveling, immorality, filthy language, and dishonesty, and turn to the true God. A changed life should be followed by water baptism. Giving to the Lord, poor as they were, was an important obligation and a privilege. They took the new concept of tithing seriously and were blessed by it. A favorite verse of Scripture was Acts 2:39: "For the promise [the gift of the Holy Spirit] is unto you, and to your children, and to all that are afar off, even as many as the Lord our God shall call."

"God thought of us when He made that promise," they said happily, "because we are the 'far off' ones!" New believers would seek earnestly to be baptized in the Holy Spirit. We were thrilled when one man received the Baptism and began to speak in English, a language he had never heard! He was praising the Lord, thanking God for sending Jesus, and saying, "Jesus is coming back soon!"

The Lisu believers loved to testify of what the Lord had done for them. In simplicity they took God at His word the way they understood it and got results.

The accounts they gave were sometimes amusing, but always inspiring. They had read in James 5:14 about the practice of anointing with oil when praying for the sick. One day Ao Ma found a woman weeping dejectedly. "My cow is dying. I was plowing the field when it fell down sick and could not get up. It was all I had. Now I have nothing left."

"Stop crying," Ao Ma encouraged. "We can pray to God to heal it. Go quickly and get some oil."

Ao Ma took the walnut oil and poured the whole bottle over the head of the dying cow. Then she prayed. The cow shook its head and stood up—healed! With a heart full of thanks, the woman resumed plowing the field.

A man who had been lame for eight years after falling from the roof of his house heard that Jesus could heal. He believed it and stood up to walk. New strength came into his crippled limbs and he was healed! He later put it this way: "There's something about the gospel story that has life and movement in it. I just *had to move,* and God gave life to my legs!"

God answered prayer in different ways. One old man came weeping and told David that his son had been drafted into the Chinese army. "I am getting old and need his help," he lamented, "but now I may never see him again." David knew this was quite likely, for some of the Lisu boys drafted were never heard of again. He prayed earnestly that God would undertake.

A couple of weeks later David was amazed to see the young man.

"How did you get here?" he asked. "I thought you were in the army."

"The Lord's grace be praised!" answered the fellow, grinning from ear to ear. "When we started training I developed a carbuncle on the back of my neck which made me lean my head forward. The officer shouted at me, 'You stupid earth boy! Can't even hold your head up! Get out of my sight and go home!' So here I am." The carbuncle soon healed, the father rejoiced in answered prayer, and the son later became a church leader in his village.

There was wonderful opportunity for mutual sharing during the Christmas and Easter conventions, which were held alternately at Wei-hsi and various Lisu villages. The people would come from far and near, bringing their own blankets, corn, rice, and bundles of wood.

A pig, a cow, or some goats would be slaughtered for meat and, during the three days, about a thousand meals would be served. On one occasion it seemed the food went much further than was possible, and there was still some left over to take home. "Jesus multiplied it as He did the loaves and fishes!" the people said in awe.

What a time of inspiration these conventions were! Singing and praying would continue all night. The women and girls were especially grateful to have been taught the Lisu phonetic script. They drank in the preaching from God's Word, as did the men. There were also times of sorrowful confession of sin with repentance. Testimony time would continue for hours. Many told of wonderful healings.

Some of the testimonies showed how God himself was causing the believers to grow in faith and in doctrine as they responded to His dealing with them. In their simplicity they learned lessons in spiritual truth from things that happened to them.

One man's testimony concerned tithing. "I didn't want to give one-tenth of my sheep to the Lord, and in my heart I refused to do so. Suddenly a disease struck the sheep and eight of them died. I repented and began to tithe. Now God is blessing and the ewes are bearing lambs. My flock is increasing!"

A woman told how she had decided to tithe her eggs. "God blessed and the hens laid well," she related. "I started for the chapel with the eggs in the basket strapped to my back. Then the devil began to put thoughts in my head. He said, 'You don't have to take those eggs to the chapel today. They are extra big ones and will fetch a good price in the market. You can use the money to buy salt and tea. Then you can make up the tithe later.' I had just decided to do that when suddenly I tripped on a root of a tree extended across my path, and down I went. Gone were the eggs, and gone was the blessing I would have received from giving them! I learned my lesson."

A more severe lesson was learned by a young man about church attendance and honoring the Lord's Day—taught by the Lisu leaders as being essential. Lou was on his way to church with a friend one Sunday. But when he saw some bear tracks he changed his mind and the two went bear hunting instead. Soon they spotted a bear.

Lou took careful aim with his Lisu crossbow. "Zing" went the bamboo arrow and down went the bear.

Calling to his friend, he pulled his long knife from its scabbard at his belt. But before he could kill the bear, it suddenly sprang up and attacked him, leaving him terribly mauled and bleeding. He would have died if some travelers hadn't come that way. His friend persuaded them to help carry Lou back to Wei-hsi. I stitched up the wounds as best I could and we prayed fervently for his recovery. Miraculously, he survived, but not without terrible scars.

"Do not do as I did," Lou now admonished the people. "Put God first in your life or you will be sorry!"

A sobering warning was sounded on the danger of compromise through the tragic experience of one old man. He had professed Christ some years before but never seemed to grow in grace. Among other things, he was not willing to give up his tobacco pipe. One day, as he returned from a trip to get tobacco, he was smoking his bamboo pipe, which was about a foot long. He stumbled and fell; the pipe pierced the roof of his mouth. He managed to get home, but lived just long enough to call on God for forgiveness of sins.

Because people who had practiced spirit worship were now worshiping God, we sometimes came face-to-face with satanic opposition. One young man suddenly cried out that three demons were coming toward him. Then he grabbed his father in a death grip. It took three other men to restrain him as we prayed. Through the mighty power of the name of Jesus the demons were cast out. This episode also had resulted from compromise. The father had professed to be a Christian but had not gotten rid of his demon altar; he still feared the demon. Now he burned it all, and four other families in the village followed suit.

In one village, a song leader led the singing with gusto. It was a favorite activity. "You see," he declared jubilantly, "once I could not sing because I could not talk. Neither could I hear. Then the 'Jesus people' came my way. They prayed for me, and God opened my ears and loosed my tongue! Is it any wonder that I love to sing and praise the Lord!"

At La Pa Shan (Western Mountain), one of the larger villages, the old Christian chief's elderly wife lay dying. Relatives had been summoned and many friends had gathered. David, Ruth, and Ao Ma also had come to give help and comfort.

It was a Lisu custom to feed all who came for the funeral. Preparations had been made for the feast and all was in readiness. It was only a matter of time before the old woman, already in a death coma, would pass away.

Ao Ma, a woman of action, suggested, "Why don't we go ahead and start preparing the food *now* while we wait?" The chief agreed. So they killed the goat and chickens and began preparing the meat, along with corn, cabbages, and turnips. Long boards were set up as tables. Some people sang and prayed while others busied themselves with the cooking. A big iron pot of broth simmered on the fire, sending forth an appetizing aroma.

Suddenly someone called excitedly, "Beh Sse Ma [the chief's wife] is moving! She is coming to! She is trying to say something!"

Quickly her daughter was at her side, listening to her in astonishment.

"Can I have some of that soup?" the dying woman repeated faintly. It took a few moments to comprehend what was happening. Then a bowl of broth was brought and gently held to her lips as family members helped her take the nourishment.

"Perhaps it is not her time to die!" said Ao Ma. "Let's pray to God to heal her!" As they prayed, a miracle happened. The woman sat up as she received divine strength into her emaciated body. Family members helped her over to the table, where she joined with the others in partaking of the food prepared for her funeral! The funeral feast became a celebration of thanksgiving to the Lord God for her healing.

As a result of this miracle a great spiritual awakening occurred in that village. Sixty families turned to the Lord in repentance and faith. The La Pa Shan church grew to three hundred members. The chief and a fine elder, Chi P'i P'a, became its leaders.

As the Lisu believers went out evangelizing the lost, praying for the sick, and teaching the believers, God worked with them. He used many marvelous proofs of His power to reveal himself in love to these people who were isolated from civilization and largely illiterate. The good news of the gospel was taken from person to person throughout that rugged, inhospitable, mountainous terrain. With persevering faith and endurance, these servants of the Lord battled forces of nature and spiritual darkness to strengthen and develop the Lisu tribespeople into a well-grounded ongoing fellowship of believers to the glory of God.

---

[1]Mark 16:20

Lisu convention at Wei-hsi

Noon meal, Lisu style, at
the Wei-hsi mission

18

No Greater Love

"Pao Mu'sze, you don't mean that we are going to take Ma Tze P'a along, do you?" David looked at me in amazement.

"Why not?" I asked as I packed my bedding into a large bundle. "I feel that he will be useful to us on the trip."

"But he is the biggest thief and gambler this side of the Mekong!" insisted David. "He is well-known for his lies and deceit. He'll steal half our stuff and disappear before we know it! Why don't we take someone else instead?"

David and I did not disagree often, but on this matter we did.

"Ma Tze P'a has expressed interest in the gospel. I feel I can talk to him as we travel. Besides, he is one of the best load carriers and mountain guides we know of. You said that yourself."

"Well, all right," conceded David, "but I'm afraid we'll be sorry."

I smiled inwardly. It seemed our national co-workers were sometimes harder on their people than we were. But then, they did know their own people better. What if David's fears proved true? We would have a serious problem on our hands while traveling. Yet, the man did seem sincere in his interest in the Scriptures.

Our trip and discussion were occasioned by an invitation from a group of tribesmen who had come to the mission station some weeks earlier. The Nung tribe had requested us to come and teach the Word of God to their people. They also wanted to purchase one hundred Gospel portions in the Fraser Lisu script. The men had walked a month's journey to reach us. Would we come?

David and I felt the challenge of the invitation. We knew, however, it would mean a long, arduous trip over formidable mountains, crossing both the Mekong and Salween Rivers and passing through dangerous jungle territory into upper Burma. We would need a group of the strongest and bravest of men to carry the extra loads of gospel literature and salt and tea with which to barter for food. We could not risk taking shirkers or thieves; stolen supplies would mean critical shortages. Again, the question came up: Should we take Ma Tze P'a along? As I prayed about it the Spirit strongly urged me to include him in our party. I assumed it was more for his sake than anyone else's.

With difficulty I said good-bye to Ada and the three small children. We would be unable to communicate while I was away—a period of at least three months. But off we went, each man with his load to carry.

Ma Tze P'a proved to be very helpful. He was always the first to begin the chores when we set up camp for the night. Each evening by the light of a kerosene lantern we shared the Word of God with the men. Ma showed genuine interest in spiritual matters, but David was still skeptical about him.

Five days later our party arrived at Shang P'a where the Clifford Morrisons ministered. There we participated in services to which the Lisu of the Salween Canyon gathered by the hundreds. The time of blessing and fellowship was thoroughly edifying.

The second day of our stopover Clifford noticed his watch was missing. David whispered to me that evidence pointed to Ma. I felt heartsick.

Just before we were to continue our journey, Clifford appeared, his face wreathed in smiles. "I've found my watch. I must have dropped it inside the pulpit, just out of sight, when I was preaching."

What a relief! Now Ma was cleared of blame.

Our journey led us over a mountain pass of seventeen thousand feet. At night we took shelter in rocky caves, warding off the elements and wild animals with continuously burning fires. Our hardiest men groaned over some of the tortuous, steep climbs. We traversed several snow-covered passes and pushed through areas of dense jungle.

One night as Ma Tze P'a and I sat by the fire, he said, "Mu Sze [Pastor], I want to become a 'Jesus follower' like you are. Can you show me the way?"

My heart leaped! Here was the opportunity I had been waiting for. Clearly and simply, I explained the way of salvation to this notorious thief and gambler. David joined us in prayer. We then taught Ma how to pray. After a while, his face took on a radiance. "I feel new inside," he said with an expression of wonder and joy.

"That's just it," we explained. "When you are saved in Christ, you are a new person."[1]

Passing over a high range between China and Burma, we came to a raging mountain stream without a bridge of any kind. We had no choice but to ford it. Holding hands, we waded out up to our waists. The current was strong. In midstream one of the men stumbled; we watched helplessly as a crucial supply of foodstuffs was swept down the river. We struggled on to the other side.

What should we do now? Would we make it to the tribes who had requested that we come with the gospel? To return home would be as difficult as pressing on. We turned to God's Word for hope and comfort, and then pushed forward. We still had the salt and tea for bartering. That afternoon one of the men shot a monkey with his bow and arrow; that night we ate monkey meat—not so bad when it's all you have!

Days of hard travel followed. We came to flat jungleland so dense that we lost our trail more than once. Monkeys screamed in the trees; bright-colored birds flew about. Along the path in countless numbers the small but dreaded leech lay in wait. Raising up on their tails, these black bloodsuckers would wave back and forth, ready to fasten themselves to a passing foot, arm, or neck. So tightly did they cling that they had to be cut away or burned off. Much of the way I walked ahead since my high-topped boots gave me better protection than the straw sandals worn by members of our party.

Late one afternoon as daylight was fading we still had not found a place of shelter for the night. Tired and hungry, we prayed, "Lord, help us to find our way and lead us to a place where there's food and shelter."

Just then I stopped short. Right in front of me, coiled up on the path, was a huge python. Awakened, it uncoiled in a flash, hissed, and came slithering toward me. In panic I called out to God. Just then, for no apparent reason, it turned its head and slid off in another direction. I could see that it was a good seven to eight feet long!

Once again the Lord had delivered us. Breathing a prayer of thanksgiving, we moved on, slowly.

Just when our strength was all but gone, we broke through into
a clearing. The sight of a hut on the far side lifted our spirits and
spurred us on. Our calls received no response, so we lit a lantern
and entered.

To our joy we found a good supply of corn on the cob hanging
from bamboo poles. Surely God had provided for our desperate
need! I bowed my head in heartfelt thanks. "Come," I said, "let's
eat and settle here for the night. If anyone shows up we will pay
for the corn with some salt."

Our famished party needed no second invitation. The men kindled
a fire and prepared the corn. Then we drank tea, ate boiled corn,
and lay down to sleep.

The next day a search of the area brought us to a circle of huts.
Seeking out the headman to pay our respects, we found him to be
rather wild-looking and unkempt, dressed in a loin cloth. But he
received us cordially.

"Are you the pastors our tribe sent for some time ago?" he asked.

"Yes," we replied. "Are you of the Nung tribe?"

"Yes. Our village is the first of quite a few Nung villages in this
area."

We had arrived!

"Stay here with us and teach us the gospel," the headman continued.

Thankfully we accepted his hospitality, and rested.

The next evening a large crowd of people gathered. The people
were primitive, isolated, and poverty-stricken, yet surprisingly in-
telligent. David and I took turns preaching and teaching in Lisu. A
bright young man who had learned the Lisu script interpreted for
us into the Nung dialect. He helped to explain the Scriptures and
teach the songs to his fellow tribespeople. The villagers listened
eagerly and asked questions. None of them had ever heard the
gospel.

A happy month went by as we traveled from one Nung village to
another, preaching, teaching, and praying with the tribespeople
(among whom were also some Lisu).

We lived on parched corn, red rice, pigeon-size eggs, and tropical fruit. When we could, we fished in the streams.

The weather was hot, humid, and wet when tropical rains came. Mosquitoes at times were so thick that even the netting above my camp cot did not keep them out. Leeches latched on to our skin and sucked our blood. Physically I was weakening. Then, with the gospel seed so newly sown, I took sick with a burning fever. It worsened despite quinine pills and all the care I could give myself. I had contracted typhoid fever.

David became alarmed, wondering what to do. Should he and the party try to take me through the jungle to Fort Hertz, the British military outpost? Or should they make the month's trip back over the mountains to Wei-hsi? A village chief informed them that the jungle fever would be worse in the plains on the way to Fort Hertz than back over the mountains.

I became delirious with the fever, and from that point on my memory is nightmarish and spotty from slipping in and out of consciousness. David described it all to me later. In great distress he prayed earnestly, "O Lord God, please show us what to do! Won't you touch Pao Mu Sze and heal Him? We're on this journey for Your gospel's sake."

As he poured out his heart to God, with tears coursing down his cheeks, he felt a hand on his shoulder and heard a resolute voice. David looked up. There stood Ma Tze P'a.

"We cannot let our pastor die here! I will carry him back home to Wei-hsi."

"But you are the smallest man in our party!" said David in astonishment.

"I am strong," replied Ma. "As a boy I used to carry loads of stone for my father when he was building our house. He said I carried heavier stones and more loads than my older and bigger brother!" That decided it.

David winced as I groaned and writhed on my cot, at times asking, "Where am I? Where is my wife?"

He comforted me, saying we would return to Wei-hsi as soon as possible.

Ma Tze P'a acquired a rope from the village chief and made a sling seat in which to strap me to himself, back to back. Then, after prayer, they bade the Nung tribespeople farewell. Now began the long tedious journey back to Wei-hsi. The men, including David, took turns carrying me. They crossed streams and struggled through thick jungle, hacking their way with machetes where the path was overgrown. Ma, to the amazement of the others, carried me the longest and farthest—once over a stretch of fourteen days.

As David watched Ma struggle along the jungle path with my inert form on his back, he thought, *What a brave strong man! How I misjudged him. Now he is a dedicated believer.* Periodically he used his hip knife to cut off the leeches sucking the blood from Ma's legs.

For part of the journey the men devised a litter with bamboo poles so my weight could be shared by two men. At night they laid me near the campfire and David tenderly cared for me the best he could, feeding me broth made from a few fowl they shot with arrows along the way.

I rallied somewhat and, supported by a man on each side, was able to walk a good part of the trip until we came to the high snow mountains. My condition worsened and the men were again compelled to carry me. David noticed blood on the trail as Ma panted up the mountainside. "What endurance you have, Ma Tze P'a!" he said. "How can you go so long with your heavy burden?"

"God helps me," replied the onetime thief and gambler. "The pastor came a long way to tell us of Jesus. I can go a little way for him. If need be I will die for him!"

At the foot of a ravine they came to a rope bridge hung across a raging river. How could they get across with such a sick man? Together they devised a method of swinging me in a basket attached to a rope. Just as the basket reached the other side where David waited to grab it, it slipped on the bank and I dropped into the river. With a cry of horror David and some men quickly rescued me and pulled my fevered body out of the swirling waters. By this time I was unconscious. David thought my end had come. He hastily exchanged my wet clothes for some others packed in my bag. Nearby was a deserted shanty; there the men built a fire to dry my wet clothes.

Then as I began to call out in delirium again, David laid his hand on my burning brow and prayed with all the fervor of his soul. "O Lord God in heaven, heal him! Keep him alive! Protect us all so we can get back safely to Wei-hsi."

An all-night vigil followed as he and Ma took turns watching me and praying. David was in agony. He thought of Alfred Lewer whom he had seen drown in the Mekong River. Was he to lose Pastor Bolton also? Could he and the men possibly get me home in time?

By morning I had rallied enough to give them some hope. David decided to run ahead to Wei-hsi and bring back some coolies to carry me in a *hua-kan,* for the men were exhausted. In the meantime, Ma once again strapped me to his back. On and on the men struggled. At last David appeared with horses and coolies. Now we could move faster. One more mountain range to cross. Then—with unutterable gratitude and relief—we reached the city of Wei-hsi at last. The incredible had been accomplished. I was home—*alive!*

Ada had been interceding in prayer. She was shocked beyond words at my condition; I did not even recognize her. Patiently she nursed me day after day, giving me quinine, which had been carefully saved for emergencies, and nourishing food.

Faithful Lisu and Chinese Christians continued in earnest prayer. The dear pastor Ch'i-tze-mei P'a spent ten days in the mountains praying for me until God gave him assurance I would live. With what joy and thanksgiving all welcomed my return to full health and strength!

During this time thousands of miles away, a woman in Carthage, New York, had been awakened by the Holy Spirit during the night "to pray for Brother Bolton in China." She spent the rest of the night in prayer until the burden was lifted. My own mother in England also had been in special prayer for me. And on my side of the world, God answered.

Ma Tze P'a had returned to his own village some distance away. Soon word came that he was seriously ill and wanted to see Ho Mu Sze (Pastor Ho).

"Does Pao Mu Sze live?" he asked weakly as David entered the room.

"Yes," said David. "He is getting better every day—thanks to you!"

"Thanks be to God," said Ma, with a relieved smile that eased the pain written on his face. "Now he can continue to tell people the good news of the gospel." His last words came haltingly, "I am so glad I helped to save his life."

He closed his eyes as in sleep. But the overtaxed heart had become still. Bending close, David perceived that Ma Tze P'a's gallant spirit had returned to his Maker.

When I learned of Ma Tze P'a's death I was moved beyond words. Truly, "greater love hath no man than this, that a man lay down his life for his friends."[2] Ma Tze P'a gave his life for me. Could I do any less for my Lord?

---

[1]2 Corinthians 5:17
[2]John 15:13

On a bamboo bridge

Leonard Bolton with Ma Tze P'a, "the biggest thief and gambler this side of the Mekong"

Among tribespeople in Upper Burma

Cliff-hugging roadway

19
Out of Death—Life!

The birth of another son brought joy to our home. With us in Wei-hsi at the time was our good friend "Auntie Jean" Wagner (nee Kucera) and her jovial new missionary husband, Harvey. Again Jean and I assisted with the delivery. We named the baby John.

Baby John became a delight in our household. A little Tibetan girl named Kuei-chih, who helped Chiang Ta-ma with some of the mission chores, was particularly enthralled with the white baby.

When John was six months old our family took a two-day trip to Chu-tien, along the Yangtze River, to visit our old missionary friends the Howard Osgoods, just back from furlough.

Our children enjoyed the rare fun of being with the Osgood children. An outing together on the banks of a nearby stream was a highlight in their young lives and a time of mutual encouragement for the parents.

But our visit was cut short when John caught a bad cold. We felt it advisable to get him back to the more suitable climate of Wei-hsi as soon as possible. Protecting the baby as well as we could, we hastily traveled home. The fever persisted. We did all we could for him. A Roman Catholic priest who now resided in Wei-hsi gave him an antibacterial injection. But John's condition did not improve. Soon we recognized the symptoms of pneumonia.

One night, we watched helplessly as he choked and struggled for breath. Then suddenly he lay still. He had breathed his last. Ada buried her head in her arms and sobbed uncontrollably. Jean gently led her from the room, whispering words of comfort and strength from God's Word.

I, too, was stunned. I went into a room alone and flung myself down on the bed. The enemy whispered, "Is it really worth it to live in this unhealthy, disease-ridden land? You almost died. Ma Tze P'a died. And now your baby son is dead."

I don't know how long the battle raged inside me, but presently a light began to penetrate the blackness, and I heard Jesus' voice once more: "Lo, I am with you."[1] Comfort came from the presence of the One who bore our griefs and carried our sorrows.

People came from all around to attend the funeral in the little chapel. Beautiful flowers graced the small coffin. Harvey preached a message of comfort while three small children wept with their parents.

Then little Kuei-chih came shyly up to Ada. Placing her hand in the missionary's hand, she said, "Didn't you tell us that dead people will live again? Why do you cry?"

"You are right, Kuei-chih. I'm not crying for baby John but for myself because I miss him. But he is with Jesus and I will see him again one day."

"I want to be a believer, too," said the girl earnestly. "Will you tell me how?"

There beside her baby's coffin Ada led the girl to a saving knowledge of Jesus. A new life was born into God's kingdom.

We buried baby John near his Uncle Alfred in a small cemetery outside the city wall. The message given at the graveside was a victorious one, reminding us of our blessed hope.

Not long after this a little Chinese girl who attended our Sunday school became very ill. Just before she died, she said, "Mother, I want a little flower in my hand like Pastor Bolton's baby had. And I want to meet Jesus." The brokenhearted mother came and talked with us. She, too, accepted the Saviour and found comfort and new life.

Shortly after this, an epidemic of measles took the lives of over two hundred children. Many of these boys and girls had attended our Sunday school regularly and had accepted Jesus as their Saviour. For this, at least, we were thankful.

Early in 1936 we were advised to take a furlough. Our sad farewells gave way to the demands of the first leg of our journey: twenty days to Kunming by horseback. (By the time we would return to Wei-hsi the next year, this travel time would be dramatically reduced—by war.) From there our mode of travel progressed: train to Haiphong, steamer to Hong Kong, and finally an ocean liner for the voyage to Italy via the Suez Canal. Our expectations for a relaxing cruise together as a family, however, were dashed when five-year-old Elsie came down with a severe case of measles. For most of the voyage mother and child were quarantined in the stern of the ship.

On the train from Italy to France my wallet containing at least £10 was stolen. When a guard slammed the heavy carriage door he almost crushed little Elsie's hand. Then, as the train sped along, Ada suddenly had a tremendous burden for prayer. On arriving in Paris we learned our train had narrowly missed an avalanche of snow which completely covered a section of track just behind us. And we had thought the perils of travel were limited to China and Burma!

After crossing the English Channel we were finally reunited with our family. One of my cousins, Margaret Jay, a schoolteacher, fell in love with our children. One day she said to me, "Leonard, it's all very well for *you* to go back to China. But these *children!* Why don't you leave them here with us in England so they can go to school?"

"Why don't *you* come with *us* and have school for them in China?" I joked. She made no reply.

Margaret was with us when we attended a meeting where the renowned English preacher Donald Gee gave an impassioned plea for consecration to the Lord. This was a turning point in Margaret's life. Soon after, she came to us and said, "I'm taking you up on that invitation. I'm going with you to China to teach your children."

"You're what!" I gasped. "You're not serious!"

"I am serious," she insisted. "I've prayed about it and I feel this is what God wants me to do."

"Do you have any idea what the living conditions are like and how you would adapt to them?" I objected. "Pray about it some more."

I wanted her to be absolutely sure this was of God for she was an unlikely candidate, being a finicky eater and having a fastidious manner. Could a "prim and proper" English lady adjust to life as we knew it in China?

Margaret did pray about it some more. Then she came to us

again. "I'm coming!" she declared. "The gifts and callings of God are not to be argued with."

We were overjoyed. This would solve the enormous problem of schooling for the children. And as a teacher, Margaret was unusually gifted.

We crossed the Atlantic to New York and finally reached Ada's home in Lancaster, Pennsylvania, for a reunion with more family and friends. A highlight of the visit was my ordination at the Eastern District Council of the Assemblies of God on April 23, 1936. Margaret came from England to join us and together we crossed to the West Coast, this time in a Model A Ford.

Ada was expecting our fifth child. For the first time she had the luxury of having her baby in an American hospital. We thanked God for a healthy boy whom we named Ralph. He was doubly loved, for God filled the vacancy felt after losing baby John.

When Ralph was two months old, in the autumn of 1936, we departed again for China. In Kunming we found suitable quarters for opening a school. I had desks made from a pattern acquired in Hong Kong. The Arthur Johnsons, with three children of their own, consented to be the first houseparents. The arrangement was that parents of students would take turns of two years each as houseparents. The school would run for nine months with a long break at Christmas, allowing time for those who had to travel a long distance home.

On arriving in Kunming Margaret was understandably shocked at many things, but she adjusted surprisingly well. She did, however, allow herself one concession: her own, if somewhat sparse, diet.

The American School, as it came to be called, also met a need for children of other missionaries. Starting with twelve pupils, it soon grew to sixteen. Featuring all grades, it was truly a one-room schoolhouse.

While busy setting up the school, I had received several letters from David Ho telling of God's continued blessing on the Lisu work. He urged me to come and baptize the many new converts and train new workers. I felt the pull to go up-country. Since baby Ralph was still so young, we decided Ada should remain in Kunming while I went ahead to Wei-hsi. She would follow later when the baby was older.

Because of the war with Japan, a road had been built linking Kunming with cities in Burma to the west and Chungking to the east. It became known as the Burma Road. What had formerly taken us thirteen days on horseback was now covered by truck in three days. But from Ta-li northward travel had not changed.

On arriving in Wei-hsi I was excited to see David and Ruth once again and to meet the new believers.

Back in Kunming Ada was anxious about Ralph. Smallpox had broken out in the area and Ralph had not been vaccinated. Three times she had taken him to an English missionary doctor, only to be told he would not vaccinate a child so young; she must wait until he was older and weighed more.

During this time two bright Chinese girls introduced by a missionary friend, Mrs. Beatrice Van Meter, had become attracted to Ada and especially to the baby. Ma Mei-ling and her sister, Ma Fei-ling, loved to visit Ada and at the same time practice speaking English. Ada used this as an opportunity for presenting them the gospel. They resisted the appeal to receive the Lord, but they did open their hearts to baby Ralph, whom they adored.

"Perhaps You can use my baby to win them to yourself, dear Lord," Ada prayed.

One day she noticed the baby had a strange fever. He was restless and couldn't sleep. When he did not improve she called the doctor. The diagnosis was smallpox, contracted perhaps when she had taken him to a Chinese clinic to be weighed, to see whether he had gained enough to be vaccinated.

The missionaries and workers of the school banded together and prayed earnestly that God would spare the six-month-old infant. Ada had to be isolated with the baby. A capable Chinese nurse who had herself survived the disease helped her care for Ralph. Mei-ling, who was preparing to be a doctor, also came at times to assist. Little Ralph's body was strong and he fought the disease, but it persisted. Ada agonized at his bedside.

One night two weeks later Ada was alone with the baby. Suddenly his small face turned blue as his body convulsed.

"Oh God, save my baby!" she cried. "He has fought it so hard. He *must* live to prove Your power and glory! Give him rest."

The convulsing suddenly stopped, his eyelids fluttered, and his face relaxed into a peaceful smile. For a moment his mother believed God had answered according to her request. Then the reality of the situation hit her. His spirit had left his body. He was at rest with Jesus.

Her body shook for an hour with great heaving sobs. "Oh God! Why didn't You answer my prayer?" her heart cried. "I don't understand! Couldn't You have spared him?"

For God "spared not his own Son, but delivered him up for us all"[2] flashed into her mind. Her thoughts turned to Jesus and how He had drunk the cup of sorrow and paid the price for the salvation of not just a few, but of the whole world. A gentle peace stole into her heart. Through her tears she whispered, "God of love, I know Your way is best. Thank You, Lord Jesus! I will praise You anyhow."

And with that, she received grace to rise again in the strength of the Lord. Quietly she kissed the baby's face and gave him back to God. Then she folded his little hands and called the other missionaries to start making burial arrangements. Pastor Albert Wood of the Assemblies of God of Great Britain conducted the funeral service.

Among the group of friends who stood within the mossy walls of the foreign cemetery outside the city wall were Mei-ling and Fei-ling. They gazed in wonder at the bereaved family. Something the Chinese girls had never seen before shone through those tears: the reality of the glorious hope of the Resurrection, the assurance of meeting again in heaven. The peace, dignity, and strength this assurance gave were vastly different from the commotion and wailing at a pagan funeral. As the coffin was lowered, Ada said softly, "Good-bye, Baby Ralph. I'll see you in the morning."

Mei-ling quietly approached Ada. Taking her hand, she said brokenly, "Now I understand what you were saying. Now I believe you spoke the truth. I want this kind of hope. I want to do as you told me and receive the Lord Jesus as my Saviour!"

Her sister indicated the same. There beside the open grave they opened their hearts to the One who is the Resurrection and the

Life. God had used our baby not in life, but in death, to bring them to the Lord.

Fei-ling later married a Chinese official and exerted a strong Christian influence in her community. Mei-ling became a prominent doctor. In her clinic for women and children she lovingly ministered to both the physical and spiritual needs of her people, leading many into the way of hope and life in Christ Jesus.

When I heard the news of Ralph's death I was grief stricken.

"She will not come back to Wei-hsi," some Chinese Christians lamented to Mary. "She will not leave her other children now. We will lose our pastor, for he will not stay without her!"

"Oh, but she *will* come!" declared Mary. "You wait and see."

Ada did not give up her burden for the Lisu. She returned to Wei-hsi, although it wrenched her heart to leave the children, especially four-year-old Irene. One comfort, however, was knowing they were in good hands; Margaret loved them as her own.

I traveled five days to meet Ada at Shih-ku, a town situated on the Yangtze River. As I enclosed her in my arms, we claimed the comfort of the Holy Spirit. We had lost two babies within three years. We committed our absent children to the Lord's care.

Back in Wei-hsi our meeting with David and Ruth was full of empathy: They, too, had known the loss of two sons. The bonds between us grew even stronger as we received comfort from each other and from the Lord.

---

[1]Matthew 28:20
[2]Romans 8:32

The Bolton Family with Baby Ralph at Home of Peace in California

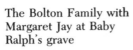

The Bolton Family with Margaret Jay at Baby Ralph's grave

20

Rope Bridge

It was good to have Ada back in Wei-hsi again. The children's absence, however, left an unaccustomed quiet. We were glad we had taken time for them—to love and comfort them, settling their small disputes, explaining our separations.

Now at meals we would sit across from each other at the table with no one to look at but each other.

"It could be worse," I said cheerfully. "We could be a lot worse to look at!"

Instead of longing for the children, we decided to think about and enjoy all the happy memories: like the way they would come to me with a broken toy and say, "Fik' it, Daddy." They believed I could fix anything.

"It's been very useful to have a handyman around," Ada commented, her crochet hook flying. "God gave you good hands, Len. Strong for fixing things, yet soft and gentle for mending people."

I looked at Ada's small, dainty hands that were always busy. "And your hands are constantly doing things to serve others," I said. "I don't know where you get all your energy."

"Same place as you," she said. We both understood well that we depended on the Lord for our strength.

But I detected something different about Ada these days. It wasn't just the sorrow of baby Ralph's death; we had been through bereavement before. Something seemed to be weighing her down, and it was not lessening with time. Her merry chuckle was gone. I let the matter rest; she would share it with me in time.

Meanwhile, God was blessing the work among the Lisu. Since its beginning in 1921 with Alfred Lewer, the number of baptized believers in nine villages in just the Wei-hsi district totaled over a thousand. Four other districts also had developed churches. The strength of growth was in whole families coming into the churches under the leadership of their village elders. Some villages had become almost entirely Christian. We taught them God's Word but did not try to change their customs if they did not conflict with Scripture. In their culture, they were still Lisu.

Believers were hungry for spiritual truth. Some men traveled for as long as three weeks to receive teaching at short-term Bible schools we conducted in Wei-hsi. Ada busied herself teaching many classes. Out of these sessions came men who developed into church leaders. These leaders then taught and screened new converts, putting them through a testing period before permitting them to be baptized and extending the "hand of fellowship" to them. They knew the sins and weaknesses of their own people. Should a convert slip back into old sinful habits, he was exhorted to repent. If he refused to repent, the hand of fellowship was refused to him; he could not partake of the Lord's table. With such measures of discipline exercised by their own leaders, scriptural standards were maintained among the Lisu.

We ministered principally in the Wei-hsi Upper Mekong region. To the southwest of us the Clifford Morrisons pioneered among the Black Lisu of the Upper Salween River area. In villages nestled along these great river canyons and along their tributaries, extending westward into the China-Burma border region, many people turned to the Lord. As the work spread far and wide, over mountain and jungle territories, teaching and grounding believers in the Word of God was a continual need.

One day some villagers from across the Mekong River arrived, requesting us to come to the district of Chia Lo and baptize over a hundred converts. This time David, Jonah, Ruth, Ada, and I set out together on muleback. After two days' journey we came to the river where several large round-bottom dugouts were secured along the bank.

"Just look at that river!" Ada gasped, gazing at the swirling whirlpools and eddying currents. "It's just too full and swift to cross. It would be suicide to try!"

"Don't worry, Sze-mu [pastor's wife]. The boatmen are experts with the current," David assured us calmly. "They can take us across safely even with the river as high as this."

Together with our mules and baggage, we went across with the dugouts tied together as one boat. The ride was turbulent, but we reached the other shore in one piece, praising the Lord!

Lisu believers welcomed us at the river bank. Then began the steep climb, too steep to ride our mules. As we struggled up the trail, I marveled at Ada's perseverance. When we rested, she told me (between gasps) that the Lord had kept her going with a song:

> *Bear the news to every land,*
> *Climb the steeps and cross the waves;*
> *Onward! 'tis our Lord's command;*
> *Jesus saves! Jesus saves!*

The welcome that awaited us at the village made the difficult trip worthwhile. The Chia Lo district had opened up during our previous furlough. Now converts wanted to follow the Lord in baptism.

That evening Lisu came from all over the mountain. We had a wonderful time worshiping the Lord together. They sang exuberantly such hymns as "Bringing in the Sheaves," "No Night There," and "Happy Day." Not long before, they had sat in spiritual darkness; now they walked in Christ's marvelous light. They continued to sing after the service and throughout the night until the mountains rang with the praises of God.

One man had traveled more than five miles to attend the service. When someone suggested that since it was past midnight they should get some sleep, he replied, "I slept for over forty years before I heard about Jesus. I've slept enough; I want to stay awake and hear more about this wonderful gospel and sing its songs."

The next morning, Sunday, it rained. Nevertheless, about two hundred Lisu came for the service. A baptismal pool had been prepared in which we baptized eleven believers. As some of them came out of the water the Spirit of the Lord fell upon them.

We spent several days in various villages preaching and teaching and personally instructing the people.

Then the day arrived for the big baptismal service. Filing down to a valley, people came from all around. Just as David and I were about to enter the stream dammed up for the occasion, a five-foot snake was discovered. After it had been caught and killed, we waded into the icy water. It didn't take long before my teeth began to chatter audibly and my feet grew numb with the cold. Since there were over eighty converts to baptize, David and I periodically came out of the water to drink hot tea and to warm up by the big fire on the bank. Many of the Lisu had no change of clothing so they stayed by the fire to dry off. Their glowing faces, exultant singing, and exuberant praises to the Lord were reward indeed for our discomfort.

We returned to the village for a Communion service. What a sight to see the believers on their knees before the Lord in worship, weeping and thanking God for Jesus!

A healing service followed. Many sick people came for prayer. As we anointed them with walnut oil, the power of God came upon them and in their simple faith God healed them. Some of the believers had large goiters on their necks. In a couple of instances we witnessed the actual healing of the goiters. These healings encouraged others to trust God.

Radiant testimonies followed. One woman told how she had prayed for a very sick child and he was marvelously healed. Another told of answered prayer in the birth of a long-awaited son—a choice blessing in Lisu culture. Their testimonies were interspersed with songs, which were sung from large song sheets or from thumb-worn songbooks.

Because of the rain, we were anxious to get back across the Mekong. However, some of the Lisu pleaded with us to go farther inland to another village and baptize believers there. We found that twenty more were ready to follow the Lord in baptism. On this trip we had now baptized one hundred twenty converts. Our final service in the Chia Lo district was held under a brush arbor, which gave us some protection from the rain.

After bidding the people farewell we descended to the Mekong River. Because of the heavy rains, the path was treacherously muddy. When we reached the river it was, as we had expected, in full flood stage. No dugouts could possibly cross the dangerous waters now. That meant the rope bridge.

This ingenious method of crossing was devised by the tribespeople and Tibetans to span the great rivers at strategic points where the canyon sides were close enough together. Bamboo or cane strips were twisted into long strands, then intertwined into a very thick rope, or cable, up to four hundred feet long. This was suspended over the chasm, each end—one usually higher than the other— secured firmly to a large tree trunk or a strongly imbedded cypress post. Unfortunately the cable rotted quickly, having to be replaced periodically.

A semicylindrical slider carved from hardwood fitted over and slid along this cable. Secured over the top of the slider and threaded through carved slots on each side were two sets of long leather thongs. One of these was tied to the person's legs to form a swinglike seat, sometimes equipped with a small board on which to sit. The other was tied around the waist or shoulders. Thus secured, the passenger grasped the slider with both hands and pushed off from the platform, being careful not to touch the cable as gravity hurtled him to the lowest point of the cable. There he would come to a stop, dangling above the river.

Then the passenger had to "monkey" up the cable to the other side. This was done by grasping the cable ahead of the slider and pulling hand over hand, at the same time pushing with the feet on the cable behind the slider. It was hard enough to pull oneself up, let alone to tow a load, as the tribesmen often had to do. The task became even more difficult when the cable had been greased with yak butter by Tibetan travelers.

We watched as one of the first men climbed the tree to the platform, roped himself in, then let himself go. Off he zoomed until, dwarfed in the distance, he hung with nothing but water beneath him. Then he pulled himself a little toward the other side and waited while a mule was tied onto another slider and pushed off. Down slid the mule, mouth gaping, tail flying, hoofs flailing. The man worked his way toward the mule and attached a rope to the animal's slider; that done, he pulled himself to the other side, along with the rope. Then with help from others, he pulled the animal up. He then returned over the cable with the extra slider. One by one the six animals plus our loads were taken across. This took many hours.

All too soon it was my turn. That I had crossed over a rope bridge before was of little comfort. This time, intending to take some pictures, I fastened my camera to my side. Far below, like a drooling monster, the river waited hungrily. It took tremendous willpower to push off. I had declared that I didn't need an assistant to help me up the other side, but I found myself praying in panic as my strength gave out. I barely made it up the last few feet; hands reached out to help me up onto the bank. Then, to my chagrin, I realized I had forgotten to take any pictures.

Now it was Ada's turn. This was the first time she had crossed on a rope bridge. I held my breath. In the distance I saw her wave to me. Then like a toboggan down a steep snowbank, down she slid; there she dangled above the raging river. A man went down from my side to attach a rope with which to pull her up. She waved again and I thought, *Why, she has more courage than I do!*

Then, almost too late, I remembered to start my movie camera rolling.

Two nights later we stopped at a Chinese inn for the night. Ada was crossing the courtyard when she noticed one of the inn's watchdogs, a large black wolf-dog, walking nearby. Suddenly, with no warning, she felt a searing pain as the dog sunk his sharp teeth into her heel. She cried out and I ran to her aid. After treating the wound with antiseptic, we prayed earnestly that no infection would set in. We were thankful that we were only a day's journey from home.

Halfway back to Wei-hsi the next day, when we stopped to cook our noon meal, it became necessary for me to change mules. To my annoyance I found that a new strap, which I had put on my saddle before we began our trip, lacked enough holes to buckle it tightly.

"Good night!" I exclaimed in English. "Now for want of an awl the strap is lost!"

David did not understand much English, but he caught part of my remark. "Why do you say 'good night' when it is day?" he asked innocently.

Ada chuckled in her old merry way. Then she explained that it was an American expression of surprise or frustration. David did not fully understand this, but he produced a nail with which to make a hole in the leather strap.

Back at Wei-hsi we rested. The Lord answered prayer for Ada's foot, and apart from the soreness, she suffered no ill effects. She had her chuckle back and was lighthearted again.

"Crossing that rope bridge must have done you good," I said to her one night. "You have been so much happier since then."

"Not the rope bridge," she corrected. "I was sore for two weeks after that! But that experience helped me cross another bridge—in my spirit." She went on to explain, "There was something in my heart that was robbing me of my joy and peace. I was brooding over the doctor's refusal to vaccinate Baby Ralph. Resentment began to grow until I knew it would harm me and others too. But I still kept thinking about it.

"When I made myself let go to cross the rope bridge, I realized that in the same way I should make myself let go of the resentment. Then the Lord would come to meet me and pull me across. I did let go, committing it all to Him. He has been helping me across by enabling me to forgive and live in victory again."

Some time later I started an another journey into Burma to visit the remote Nung and Lisu people I had contacted on previous trips. It was always hard for Ada to see me leave. She remembered how near death I had come on my first trip. But in her consecration to the Lord she did not try to hold me back. We planned for her to visit the children at their school while I was away.

Once more David and I sowed gospel seed among those primitive people. We covered some seven hundred miles on foot in the three months of travel. Then I became ill again and had to return home. Since Ada was in Kunming with the children, Mary cared for me, sending word to Ada to return immediately. A CIM missionary doctor in Ta-li, Dr. Stuart Haverson, traveled the ten days' journey to Wei-hsi to treat me—a sacrificial kindness we would always remember. He advised me to take no more such long trips. But I could not forget that beyond the rope bridges were many who still needed the gospel.

David Ho and Leonard Bolton baptizing Lisu convert

Leonard Bolton with snake caught before baptismal service

David Ho in the "swing-like seat" at the lowest point of a rope bridge over the Mekong River, and "monkeying" up to the other side

"One by one the six animals plus our loads were taken across."

21

Houseparents

The Chinese-Japanese War moved steadily westward. As China's eastern provinces fell to enemy control, refugees poured into Yunnan Province. Up-country, we listened to news on our battery-operated radio, charged by our waterwheel-powered generator.

We were concerned about the children at school in Kunming. Then a letter arrived from Margaret. She wrote that one day they had heard the drone of approaching airplanes. The children ran outside to watch a fleet of nine silver planes sparkling in the sunshine as they flew in formation. Exclamations of admiration suddenly changed to cries of alarm as bombs began falling from the planes. Sirens wailed and everyone dived for shelter in trenches. When the attack ended, they thanked God that no bombs had fallen near the school. Other parts of the city, however, suffered much destruction.

The Japanese air raids continued. We decided to end the school term early to ensure the children's safe return to their parents for the Christmas vacation. Then the school would be moved to Ta-li, away from the bombings. After all the others had left, the Wagners, Osgoods, our three children, and Margaret traveled in a battered bus toward Ta-li along the Burma Road. The bus driver careened recklessly around the zigzag turns, which did not have guard rails. At noon on the second day they smelled something burning. The driver stopped and yelled, "Out! Everybody out! The engine's on fire!"

Out through the windows the smaller children were passed, while the older ones jumped out the back. The damage was not too bad, however, and after a while the driver ordered everybody in again to continue the journey. On the third day they reached Ta-li with indescribable relief.

Ada and I traveled to Ta-li to meet the children and bring them home to Wei-hsi. In joy and thankfulness we embraced them. We had been separated from them by a fifteen-day journey for each nine-month school year. The Christmas convention with the Lisu and the family celebrations were especially meaningful that year. An added joy was having Margaret Jay join the Lewers and us.

My surprise for the Christmas dinner was two wild ducks I had managed to shoot with one shot. The cook dressed and roasted them to an appetizing finish, and brought them in proudly. We started eating with enthusiasm.

Then forks dropped. Exclamations of "Ugh!" came from the children. Tastebuds anticipating duck were not prepared for a strong fishy flavor. We liked fish, and we liked duck—but not fishy duck. I decided it would have been wiser and easier to stick to domestic fowl.

Ada's surprise, however, made up for the disappointing duck. She had sent someone into the mountains for a basketful of snow. Mixing the snow with salt and saved-up cream, she had made ice cream.

In Ta-li the Harvey Wagners, houseparents following the Arthur Johnsons, leased a fine property for the school. Its adjoining lots with a connecting gate provided adequate facilities for both school and living quarters. The yards had a variety of trees, enough space for vegetable and flower gardens, and a playground. The CIM missionary home, church, and hospital nearby meant medical facilities were readily available. On Saturdays and holidays, the children played with the doctors, nurses, and missionaries who also enjoyed the diversion. With a beautiful view of the mountains, snow-capped during part of the year, and the Erh-hai Lake nearby, the school had found an ideal location in coming to Ta-li.

In 1940 Ada and I were asked to take our turn as houseparents. Mary had returned to Wei-hsi after leaving her two daughters in Hong Kong where they were attending a British school. So we commended the work to her and David and Ruth and reluctantly took leave of the Lisu.

I moved our equipment for generating electricity from Wei-hsi to Ta-li. I installed the unit in a water mill located near the school.

Now we could have electric lights and I could use some power tools. My ability as a handyman was in constant demand.

From a table for two, Ada and I went to a table for twenty: twelve boarding students and eight day students. We were mother, father, pastor, nurse, playmates, rule-enforcers, peacemakers, comforters, and spiritual counselors.

In addition to mothering, Ada managed the housekeeping, meals, guests, and accounts. Wang Sze-fu, our cook from Wei-hsi, manned the kitchen. Chiang Ta-ma, also from Wei-hsi, helped to draw water and to boil it for drinking and to heat it for washing. She and some other women did all the washing by hand.

Margaret was respected as "Miss Jay" in class and loved as "Auntie Margaret" outside class. In addition to teaching the three *R*s, she involved *all* the children in learning to play the pump organ or piano, to paint with water colors, to write poetry, to act in plays, and to read and appreciate good literature. Outings, considered a part of education, were enjoyed with relish. It was a unique setup: The American School with an English teacher, using the latest State-side textbooks, for students of several nationalities—in China!

Our dining room table was often extended as guests came through Ta-li. Ada became acquainted with their culinary preferences and sought to please. One frequent guest, Harvey Wagner, would always peek in the kitchen to see what was for dessert, the part of the meal he loved best. One day Ada hid the dessert and served a kind of Kool-Aid drink with the meal instead of plain water. After the main course was eaten she made no move to bring in the dessert. Harvey became restless. Unable to hold back any longer, he eagerly asked Ada, "What's for dessert?"

"Oh, you drank it," she replied casually.

Harvey's face fell. Then after a good chuckle she produced his favorite dessert, homemade peach-quince pie.

One special guest of the school both delighted and awed the students. Quentin Roosevelt, grandson of Theodore Roosevelt, shared his late grandfather's enthusiasm for adventure in the outdoors. With him when he stopped at the school were some rare species of musk deer he had captured in upper Yunnan. Our two watchdogs, normally let loose at night, were kept away from the cages and tied up. One night the dogs somehow got loose, broke into the cages, and killed the deer.

We were mortified! The loss was irrevocable. What could I do or say? Our apologies were profuse. But Mr. Roosevelt was magnanimous. He even donated a fine selection of books to the school library, much to Margarets's delight.

Each school day Margaret began with reading from God's Word, followed by prayer. After supper, we had devotions. On Saturday mornings, we conducted "family prayers." We sang a hymn, then covered a chapter of Scripture, each one around the circle reading aloud two verses. We took time for worshiping the Lord and praying for one another. On Sundays Margaret held a Sunday school class and made the Bible stories come alive. These spiritual touches on our lives and activities paid dividends: All the children learned to know the Lord.

Our peace was jarred again one day by warnings that Japanese war planes were coming. We quickly marched the children out of the city to hide in some fields. Hours dragged by. We had them sing and quote Bible verses to keep up their morale. The planes came, but concentrated their attack about ten miles away, at Hsia-kuan on the Burma Road. Relieved, we trudged back home, thankful to have been spared.

The shortage in our supplies of food, shoes, and clothing was becoming acute. Replenishing them seemed promising when one Dr. Taylor offered me transportation to Rangoon if I would serve as driver and mechanic of his Dodge truck. That meant the "back door" to China, the Burma Road. All other supply lines had been cut off by the Japanese.

Used to bring reinforcements for Chiang Kai-shek's military forces, the Burma Road was a target of enemy attacks. Wreckage of bombed and burned trucks marked our way. Less obvious was the wreckage of vehicles that had simply gone off the road and over a cliff. Bridges were unsafe. At one place where the bridge over the Mekong had been completely destroyed, we crossed on a makeshift pontoon bridge, planks placed over empty steel barrels lashed together. We traveled much of the way by night, taking cover during the day.

Coming into a thick jungle area we decided to park in a hidden spot and get a good night's rest. I set up my cot near the road. Dr. Taylor slept in the cab. During the night I was awakened by a rumbling sound and a low growl. In the darkness I saw two large luminous eyes looking right at me. A mountain lion or a tiger? I broke out in a cold sweat and reached for my gun—which had been left in the truck! Just then, another rumble, and a large boulder came rolling down, barely missing me. And with it, the eyes disappeared. I made one big dash for the truck and jumped in right on top of Dr. Taylor. His turn for a jolt! So much for a peaceful night's sleep.

Eventually, after three changes of springs and many tire repairs, we drove into Rangoon. Consulting my list—thirty pairs of shoes, clothing, some bicycles, medical and school supplies, and food—I did my shopping. Dr. Taylor acquired a new truck, to be driven back by Dr. Logan Roots, a medical missionary. Most of my supplies went into the new truck. The old one would carry the food.

Although still in Burma, we were more than halfway home when we drove through Lashio, where we would pick up the Burma Road.

Beyond the city, as I rounded a bend, I was horrified to see the new truck in flames. Dr. Roots had been able to jump out, but everything else went up in smoke. We learned later that an enemy saboteur, disguised in the orange robes of a Buddhist monk, had thrown a firebomb into the back of the truck. Heartsick, but thankful to be alive, we prepared to go on. We salvaged what we could, including the engine, and hired an army truck, which I drove. From then on I spent my nights sleeping on the army supplies it contained—three tons of TNT!

After several days without further incident we arrived safely in Ta-li. The children gathered around in anticipation, only to learn there were no new notebooks, clothes, or shoes. Everyone felt the loss of the supplies. However, some gifts I had for the children compensated a little, and the food was a blessing. We claimed the promise of Romans 8:28 that "all things work together for good to them that love God"—and called in a shoe repair man. He set up shop right in the yard as each child brought out his battered, worn shoes. What an array! Ada rose to the occasion by preparing some special goodies from the supply of food that had been mercifully spared. So we had a great shoe party.

At the close of the school year (November 1941) we talked of a vacation for Margaret, sorely in need of a rest and change. She was able to go with a friend of hers, Miss Morgan, to vacation in Hong Kong.

While James Andrews, our missionary friend from Li-chiang, was in Ta-li, we decided to make an exploratory trip to Ho-p'ing and the surrounding area. We found the people responsive. Since I had a desire to reach out, I was hoping to start a new work there among the Lisu. But our trip was cut short when a runner arrived breathlessly with a message from Ada: "The Japanese are coming closer. Hurry back!"

Arriving back at the school, we heard news reports that the Japanese were planning to invade Yunnan. Margaret, who had written enthusiastically about the wonderful time she was having, had been encouraged by friends to stay in Hong Kong for Christmas. We were filled with uncertainty.

Then Pearl Harbor was bombed, thrusting America into the war. The most unexpected development, however, was Japan's seizure of Hong Kong. We were stunned. What of Margaret? We heard no more news from her. Against all hope, we kept hoping.

January came, time for a new school year. But still no news of Margaret. Then we heard that all British, Canadian, and American citizens in Hong Kong had been interned by the Japanese in a concentration camp on Hong Kong Island. News filtered through that Margaret was among them. Our hearts were like lead. We attempted to continue the school with substitute teachers. But by June, the war situation had become such that the Ta-li school, so ideal while it lasted, had to come to an end.

Miss Margaret Jay, teacher

Reading papers from the Gospel Publishing House, Springfield, Missouri—six months old!

Students at the Ta-li American School

Shoe-mending day at the American School in Ta-li

Travel to and from school

In Wei-hsi without the children

Margaret starting her vacation trip to Hong Kong

22
War Upheavals

Missionaries had been advised to leave China. Kunming, originating point of the Burma Road, seethed with war activities. Chinese military resistance was being reinforced with supplies brought through the "back door." The Flying Tigers, a volunteer group of American fliers under retired Air Force General Claire Lee Chennault, flew their missions out of Kunming, providing an effective air defense for southwestern China.

We now faced the dilemma of what our family should do. Should we leave China or should we take our children with us back to Weihsi? Could we continue our ministry while waiting out the war? Would that be wise? How long would the war last? It had been six years since our last furlough. Many questions plagued us. We prayed for divine guidance.

We decided to evacuate up-country, hoping it would be possible to remain in China. With refugees pouring into Yunnan, travel was difficult. Unable to hire horses, we took with us what we could and boarded a junk sailboat to the north end of Erh-hai Lake. At Dragon's Head Pass we were able to hire three riding horses for the five of us. The girls and Ada rode the horses until I came down with a fever and dysentery and needed to ride, then the girls took turns walking. My thirteen-year-old son, Bob, prayed for me and I was strengthened. He refused to take a turn riding and walked the entire trip of over a hundred miles in straw sandals.

At Li-chiang the James Andrews family welcomed us warmly. We shared precious fellowship with them and ministered among the believers. While there, we listened to the news by shortwave radio. We then realized the necessity of leaving China, especially for the sake of the children. We started out for Kunming, hoping to get air transportation out of China over the Himalayan mountains to India. The usual exits through Hong Kong and Rangoon already had been cut off.

Travel to Ta-li was even worse than before. The rainy season had begun. Trails were treacherous. A cholera plague was killing thousands. Passing through towns and villages, we saw row after row of white handprints along the walls and doors—supposedly to ward off the evil spirits bringing the dread disease. We saw coffin after coffin being taken out for burial.

One evening, cold, wet, and exhausted, we came into a deserted village. We kept calling, "Is anyone around?"

Finally we saw a man approaching. He said he lived on a neighboring farm and so far had escaped the disease. He showed us an upstairs room where we could sleep. As it grew dark, we could hear the calls of jackals and wolves, no doubt preying on the dead outside the compound walls. After putting the children to bed on their cots, Ada opened her Bible and read, "There shall no evil befall thee, neither shall any plague come nigh thy dwelling."[1] We humbly bowed our heads, claiming God's promise and giving thanks for His protection.

Leaving the cholera-infested area, we came at last to Ta-li. We arranged for our cook, Wang Tze-fu, and Chiang Ta-ma to return to Wei-hsi, then concluded business concerning the leased properties. Next we sought a way to travel to Kunming, but all trucks had been commandeered for war service. The situation was desperate.

At Hsia-kuan I met Dr. May, who worked with an American team of medical volunteers. He had an ambulance and was about to return to Kunming. I asked if he could squeeze in our family. He showed me five bullet holes in the roof of the ambulance. "Three of my team were killed when enemy planes strafed my ambulance on the way here," he told me. "They disregarded the giant Red Cross painted on the roof. But if you are willing to take the risk I can squeeze you in."

We had no other choice. I thanked him. Since the Red Cross emblem was no protection, we covered the red paint with mud to camouflage the vehicle. We did encounter enemy fire during the three-day trip, but the Lord marvelously protected us.

At Kunming we learned that only a few planes had not been destroyed. The Lord brought us into contact with one of Chennault's men who helped us secure passage on a China Air Transport (CAT) plane. Strapped into aluminum bucket seats on the crowded twin-engine plane, we were in danger of enemy attack. When we flew northward over the great Mekong and Salween divides, my heart was too full to speak as I gazed down at those mountains where the people we loved lived.

Flying through much turbulence, over the part of the Himalayas nicknamed "the Hump," at twenty thousand feet without oxygen we all became airsick. Later, at a lower altitude, Elsie looked down at a vast area of thick jungle. "What would happen if we crashed down there?" she asked a friendly airman.

"The tigers would eat you up, of course," he answered jovially. Her eyes grew big. Contemplating this new idea helped her forget the dangers through which we had come.

A brief stop at the military airport in Assam, in northeast India, gave us refreshing relief. We stood under the plane's wings in pouring rain while kind American airmen served us hot tea, coffee, and, of all things, a delight foreign to the children—angel food cake. As we bowed our heads in grateful thanks and praise to God, we felt He truly had given His angels charge over us to bring us safely out of war-torn China.

With deep gratitude we landed in Calcutta. Unable to take much with us when we left, we had put on many layers of clothing—which served well in the cold plane at high altitudes. Now we stepped into the steamy heat of the tropics. Nevertheless the children found it new and exciting: banana trees, palms, luxuriant tropical flowers, a modern electric tramway system, and sacred cows. Trying to enter the large Lloyd's Bank on a main street one day, I was forced to go around to the back door. A large white cow, considered sacred, was lying across the front entrance and was not to be disturbed.

While staying at the Lee Memorial Home, I became ill and had to be hospitalized, a reaction to all that had happened. After I recovered, we enjoyed fellowship with Missionary Maynard Ketcham and his national co-workers at the House of Prayer.

We crossed India by train to Bombay, where, together with forty other missionaries, we boarded the troop ship *Mariposa* on its return voyage to the States by way of South Africa. Steaming at full speed, which caused speed vibrations, we zigzagged across the Indian Ocean trying to avoid submarine attacks. Now it was Ada's turn to react to the strain. She became ill and developed a large carbuncle. Through the prayer of faith by a veteran missionary to India, James Boyce, the Lord healed her. When we stopped at Cape Town I bought her a beautiful sweater to help lift her spirits.

During the nightmarish voyage up both the South and North Atlantic oceans to New York, the missionaries prayed fervently. We were under strict blackout rules, being in constant danger of German U-boat attacks. Once our ship lurched so violently that objects everywhere went flying. We learned a torpedo had just missed us.

At last we sailed through the Narrows into New York Harbor. A serviceman's cry of "There's the Old Lady!" was accompanied by joyful shouts throughout the ship as with swelling emotions we gazed at the Statue of Liberty. On landing, the captain formally thanked the missionaries, crediting the safe voyage to their prayers.

Our family was welcomed into the home of Ada's cousin, Ada Brubaker, and her husband Thomas, who pastored a church on Staten Island. Later, we stayed with her brother's family, the Omar Buchwalters in Lancaster, Pennsylvania.

While pioneering a church in Kingston, New York, we had the rare privilege of a private American homelife for almost two happy years. As our children grew spiritually, they were baptized in water along with a nucleus of new believers. While attending Maranatha Park, a summer church camp in Green Lane, Pennsylvania, all three children received the infilling of the Holy Spirit, bringing great joy to us all. Back in Kingston, the Lord continued to bless and the church was established. But the call of China remained.

IN 1945 WE PLANNED TO RETURN TO CHINA by way of England, enabling us to visit my family. I found the constant barrage of bombings and the short supply of life's necessities had taken its toll on my parents. While we were there, Victory Day in Europe (V-E Day) was celebrated with great rejoicing.

When we found we could not proceed to China through the Suez Canal, we left the children with relatives in England and returned to America, intending to leave from the west coast. We planned for the girls to join us after we had settled in China and reopened the school. Our son, upon turning eighteen, would attend Bible college in America.

We acquired an automobile through a new missionary equipment assistance program sponsored by the youth of the Assemblies of God called Speed-the-Light. We drove all the way to the west coast, only to find we had to drive back again to board ship in New Orleans. The ship then sailed around and up the west coast, where we had gone in the first place but had not been permitted to board with our vehicle. The frustrations of war restrictions were not yet over!

Arriving in China at Shanghai, we found postwar chaos and upheaval. We teamed up with the Osgood family and Doris Marsh, a teacher from the state of Washington. Together we drove across the breadth of China to Kunming, Howard Osgood with his truck and trailer, and I with my Speed-the-Light Dodge. Again, my mechanical ability was to our advantage. The trip took fifty days and covered about three thousand miles. We took extra supplies of gasoline, spare tires and tubes, wheels, springs, other spare parts, and tools.

We found roads bombed and bridges torn up. At one place we crossed a river on a railway bridge; at others, on makeshift pontoons or improvised bridges. Shallow rivers we forded. Rain compounded our difficulties. We passed through a famine area where we had to pay exorbitant prices for food.

Many people had never seen a trailer before. As we followed Howard's truck towing the trailer behind it, we heard the people's amusing reaction all along the way. "Look!" they called out. "The big one has a baby!"

Finally in November 1945 we reached Yunnan Province, the land of our calling. We had been away for three and a half war years. Arriving in Kunming after fifty days of travel, we faced the immediate problem of accommodations; many missionaries were returning after the war. We "camped" for a while in a row of rooms with a courtyard, outside the east gate of the city.

The first order of events was to reopen the American School. Kunming was the logical place. The Lord provided a suitable walled-in compound and we moved into an existing building. Then during 1946, in a record six months, a new two-story building was constructed for a school complex and missionary home. Miss Marsh proved to be a capable and understanding teacher.

Some wonderful news brought us great excitement. Margaret had been repatriated. With help and strength from God alone, she had survived four and a half years of untold hardship and misery in the Stanley Imprisonment Camp in Hong Kong. Perhaps her birdlike eating habits had been an advantage in helping her exist on so little food for so long. Many of the prisoners did not survive. Margaret had put her creativity to work and helped to keep up morale in the camp by "teaching school" with imaginative ideas and almost non-existent equipment. Now, after a time of recuperation in England, she was returning to China. And she was bringing our daughters, Elsie and Irene, with her. What joy to be together again!

Now with two teachers, enrollment grew in a short time to twenty-eight—all that could be handled. Margaret taught the primary pupils and Doris Marsh the high school students.

Again we found ourselves houseparents and busier than ever. Extra precautions had to be taken because of post-war disease in the area, including smallpox. We missed being among the Lisu, but since God had given us this responsibility, we gave it our best. The children responded to our love, calling us Aunt Ada and Uncle Len. We enjoyed fun together on weekly outings. We also exercised discipline. One of the boys said to his mother, "When I'm naughty I have to sit by Uncle Len, and then I *have* to be good!"

Our son, Robert, far away in England, had turned eighteen. He sought to leave for America to enroll at Central Bible Institute in Springfield, Missouri, to train for missionary service. However, due to end-of-war conditions, he was unable to obtain passage to the States. Meanwhile, a notice came that he was to be drafted into the British Army. Only if he left for study in America could he be exempted. We prayed fervently.

Then we learned with thankfulness that a cancellation, timed just when Robert was at the shipping office, enabled him to get a berth and leave England. Ten days later his draft notice came, but he had already left for America. Again we thanked God for answering prayer.

As houseparents our responsibilities also included running a missionary home, with a constant flow of guests coming through Kunming after the war. Among those who stopped were Mary Lewer and her older daughter, Katherine, who had graduated from Central Bible Institute and received missionary appointment. We were happy to see this mother-daughter team and rejoiced that the Lord had called Katherine to ministry in Wei-hsi.

Our minds went back to a day at the Wei-hsi chapel when Katherine was five. After seeing our Chinese teacher, Mr. Lee, take his stand for Christ, she said to her mother, "Mama, I want you to pray with me like you and Uncle Len prayed with the teacher. I want to repent and believe in Jesus."

After we prayed with her she rose from her knees and in clear Chinese said to the congregation, "I believe in Jesus!" We felt then that God had His hand on her young life.

As Mary and Katharine started the trip up-country we longed to go with them, but the Lord had work for us to do in Kunming.

---

[1]Psalm 91:10

Ada and Leonard Bolton with Irene *(front row)*, Robert and Elsie *(back row)*, after their escape from China during World War II

23
Last Years in Mainland China

Our hands were full, very full. Care of the school and the missionary home was enough to occupy all our time. At the same time, however, we were feeling an urgency to do all we could to get the gospel out.

A chapel we opened downtown brought in a variety of people: businessmen stroking their sparse beards, mothers nursing their babies, coolies wearing faded blue clothes, and many bright young people and children. Services were held in Mandarin Chinese, but since many students now desired to hear English, we made some of the meetings bilingual. Some students also attended our Sunday school in the American School compound.

I trained several Spirit-filled young men who felt called to preach. With a battery-powered amplifier and loudspeakers on top of our Speed-the-Light Dodge we would go out into the country markets on Saturday afternoons to hold open-air meetings, enabling hundreds of people to hear the gospel. We did this also among the crowds celebrating the Chinese New Year. Our young men gave out thousands of gospel tracts.

A ministry developed among several leper camps near Kunming. Some workers and I, together with a nurse, ministered among the lepers. Many had parts of their hands, feet, and noses eaten away by the disease. They greatly appreciated the love shown, as food and clothing were given to them. Injections were administered by the nurse. Hope and joy took the place of despair as many of them came to the Lord.

To cope with the never-ending need for literature, I contacted a Chinese publisher and had many Chinese and Lisu gospel booklets and tracts printed. I also worked on the translation of a Lisu hymnbook for printing with the help of none other than John Ho, David's son. Like the Prodigal Son, he had left home, causing his parents much heartache. But through their unceasing, fervent prayer he had been brought back to the Lord, filled with the Spirit, and set aflame for God. We rejoiced to see him so eager to serve the Lord with his father.

The Holy Spirit also moved among the students in the American School during services held in the mission compound. Several received the baptism in the Spirit; gifts of the Spirit were manifested and a good foundation for spiritual maturity was laid. Many of the students later entered the Lord's work.

One of the nonmissionary students was the French consul's daughter, Arlette. Through the testimony of Margaret and our girls, she accepted the Lord and wanted to be baptized. A memorable baptismal service took place later on the banks of a waterway on the outskirts of Kunming. Included among the Chinese candidates were several missionary children and blonde-haired Arlette. Some five hundred curious onlookers gathered. As they witnessed the joyous singing and worshiping of the young people, faces and hands lifted to the skies, the holy beauty of the scene silenced any would-be scoffers.

We received an invitation for our American School students to participate with music and singing in a monthly ninety-minute program on a Kunming radio station. In this manner they witnessed to many Chinese who understood English.

In October 1947, our first conference for all of southwest China was held, with Howard Osgood as chairman. It was a time of rich fellowship; international in flavor, it included British, German, Swedish, and Finnish Pentecostal missionaries.

Ada and I were overjoyed to meet the five Wei-hsi representatives, including Katherine Lewer, David Ho, and Jonah. Our hearts overflowed.

David shared with us the Lord's blessing on the work among the Lisu. He recounted many instances of God's protection and care during the war years.

He told of a village where the Spirit of God had been moving. The devil stirred up the heathen villagers to capture a believer who had been a spirit-medium before he was saved. Angry because he was of no more use to them, they tied him to a stake, preparing to burn him alive. Word reached believers across the valley. A woman who had the power of God upon her came running. Under a mighty anointing, she preached God's Word to them. Conviction gripped their hearts, and they released the man. Many fell to their knees and, like the Philippian jailer of old, cried, "What must I do to be saved?"

When the conference was over, Katherine, David, and the Lisu pastors packed up a large supply of Lisu gospel booklets, hymn-books, and tracts. Then seated on top of a pile of luggage on a charcoal-burning truck for the first leg of the journey back to Wei-hsi, Katherine cheerfully waved good-bye. We did not realize this would be the last time we would see her. Back among the primitive villagers she ministered with ardent dedication, often with inade-quate diet and insufficient shelter from the merciless winter weather. Extending herself beyond the limits of even the vigor of her youth, her once strong body succumbed to sickness.

As she endured the combined assasult of cholera, typhoid fever, and a spinal abscess, her courageous mother watched in agony by her bedside, doing what little she could to ease the suffering. Pastor David and his wife Ruth stood vigil with her until Katherine's death. Tenderly she was laid to rest beside her father's grave in the little Wei-hsi cemetery.

With Easter again came the comfort of the risen Saviour. It was a time of spiritual harvest. Hundreds of Christians from all the churches gathered outdoors in a park among the cherry blossoms for an Easter service. Many other people milled around, listening to the message of the resurrected Christ.

Bob Pierce, founder of World Vision, Inc., came to Kunming and held a city-wide evangelistic crusade. I assisted wherever I could and used my car with the public address system to announce the meetings. Elsie played the piano in the auditorium (while rats played around her feet). When Dr. Pierce gave the altar call each night, scores of people eagerly surged forward to accept Christ as their Saviour.

I could not help thinking how the present response to the gospel contrasted with the resistance our missionary pioneers had met originally.

October 1948 saw an answer to a long-standing prayer of all the Pentecostal missionaries in Yunnan: The Ling Kuang (Holy Light) Bible Institute at last became a reality. James Baker, son of H. A. Baker, a veteran missionary in Yunnan, became the principal of the school. Two of the twenty-two students who enrolled had served as Buddhist monks in a famous temple near Kunming. A few came more than a thousand miles, from as far away as Shan-hsi Province in north-central China. They and the dean, Rev. Ku Kuai-kung, had recently escaped from Communist rule in northern China.

The formal opening took place with the convening of the second Southwest China Conference of the China Assemblies of God. Rev. Donald Gee from the British Assemblies of God shared in ministry. The conference was marked by a unity among the various missionary groups, feeling the urgency of giving the new Bible institute support and spreading the gospel while the door was still open. Already strong undercurrents of a Communist takeover ran through the land.

For some time we had been considering taking a trip back to the Lisu. David wanted us to come for the Christmas convention. But it seemed our responsibilities would not allow it. Ada was also in charge of all the accounts. With the depreciation of the Chinese dollar, figures were running into the billions! A ride to town in a ricksha now cost five hundred thousand Chinese dollars. When Mrs. Edith Osgood heard of our desire to go, she offered to substitute for Ada. So, gratefully, we made preparations to take Elsie and Irene with us. They wanted to visit once again the place of their birth.

The American consul warned us of the danger caused by Communist activity, but we felt we should get the literature to the Lisu and see them once again.

The first of December, 1948, we loaded up the Dodge with our bedding, clothes, food, six thousand Lisu booklets, and Christmas gifts for the Christians. Leaving the car at a Swedish mission station after two and a half days' travel to Hsia-kuan, we joined a hundred-horse Tibetan caravan for the rest of the way. At Ta-li, Ada and I purchased a gravestone of the famous Ta-li marble for Katherine's grave. The trip had its usual hardships, but we were thankful not to encounter any bandits. Travel with so many Tibetans was a memorable experience for our girls, especially to be offered Tibetan tea! When it was possible we camped out with the caravan at night to avoid the dirty inns.

When at last Wei-hsi came into sight the girls could hardly contain their excitement. A delegation of believers came out along the trail to meet us. Upon our arrival at the mission station, Mary welcomed us. She had prepared a delicious chicken dinner. We shared with her the sorrow of Katherine's death. Later, the girls eagerly explored the old mission house of their childhood years.

After a two-day rest we started out with a small group on mules for the last part of our trip. The two-day convention was to be held fifty miles away at La Ma Lo, ten thousand feet above sea level. The trail was no Burma Road. On the many steep climbs, too steep for staying on the mules, even our energetic teenagers needed to stop for breath.

As we struggled up one especially long, rigorous climb to a rocky crest, we suddenly heard what sounded like a heavenly choir. The first welcoming group had spotted our approach. It spurred us on with heartbeats quickened.

As we reached them, with shining faces and shouts of joy they formed a line for the "hand of fellowship." We filed by, shaking hands with each one, a mode of greeting used only by the believers among the Lisu. Farther on we met the second welcoming group. They likewise sang for us and welcomed us with a handshake and cries of "Hua Hua Le Le!" ("Peace! Peace!")

At the entrance of the village a welcome arch had been erected with special care, decorated with pine branches, rhododendrons, and wild flowers. Beyond this waited the main welcoming group, jubilantly singing the songs we had taught them. We felt like royalty as we passed through the arch and shook hands with each one in the long line. Our girls were the big attraction as the people crowded around with cries of admiration and delight.

Two hundred Lisu had gathered for this convention. Some had walked forty miles on bare feet, the women carrying their babies on their backs. Their feet bruised and bleeding, they nevertheless had a song and a smile.

The people had brought eggs and chickens to exchange for Gospel portions and picture tracts. They received the hymnbooks with special gladness.

Men had erected a large shelter with woven bamboo mats and poles. Pastor David Ho and other leaders were present to help with the services. The Lisu sang, praised, prayed, preached, and testified throughout the day. Then they formed groups around fires to keep warm and sang throughout the night. We also had periods of Bible study, and the people wanted still more.

The second day continued with the same ardor. Testimonies were remarkable. Some had suffered persecution at the hands of angry villagers. One Christian man had refused to share in the spirit worship of his village to bring rain. They threw him in an isolated prison house where, in freezing weather, he had to stand all night in water up to his ankles. Finally through the prayers of other believers he was released. Although he suffered in his feet as a result, he was full of praise to God for being considered worthy to suffer for Christ.

Others had given their lives for the sake of the gospel. One young pastor had a wonderful ministry among his small band of believers. One day, however, while he worked in his cornfield, he was attacked by a mad wolf-dog. David Ho prayed over him for weeks, but he died, leaving a family of six children. His young wife grieved inconsolably. She felt her husband could not be happy because of his terrible death.

Then comfort came through one of her children. Her small son, waking from a dream, called out, "Oh, I don't want to go back!" She asked him what he was talking about. He told her, "I have been in such a beautiful place! I saw Pa Pa and he was dressed in a fine uniform [his best idea of finery]. He was with a bright shining Man and he looked so happy!"

Since then, the young wife had been very zealous, leading the meetings in her small village and encouraging others.

A remarkable story was told by an elderly man. Although old and feeble, he, along with others of his village, had to travel over a fifteen thousand foot mountain to sell his hemp rope and buy supplies. On the return trip he suddenly became so weak he could go no farther. He appeared to be dying. His companions carried him through the snow until they came to a cave. Since he appeared to be dead, they laid his body in the cave, covered it with a goatskin, and trudged on over the mountain.

Five days later he came walking into the village and was surprised when his friends thought he was a ghost.

He told them he had awakened in the cave to find a brightly burning fire and food beside him. He ate, drank, and warmed himself. Then, feeling refreshed, he came on over the mountain, not knowing he had been lying as dead in the cave for several days! His friends felt sure an angel of God had ministered to him just as one had to Elijah.[1]

All too soon the convention was over and it was time for us to leave. We gave each believer a small but valued memento: a pencil, handkerchief, safety pins, or needles. After saddling our horses we offered a final prayer, committing them to the Lord and encouraging them to be faithful. Then they lined up to shake our hands in farewell.

The people accompanied us for some distance. But we finally had to part. As we rode away, they sang, "God be with you till we meet again." The sound followed us until we were out of earshot. I cried freely. Somehow I felt it would be a long time, perhaps not until we reached heaven, before we would meet again.

At Wei-hsi we conducted a memorial service for Katherine and set up the marble gravestone at her grave, beside those of Alfred and Baby John. We marveled at Mary's fortitude.

David accompanied us downcountry as far as Hsia-kuan, where our car was. As we prayed together, the Lord gave us the verse: "He shall not be afraid of evil tidings: his heart is fixed, trusting in the Lord."[2] I didn't understand why until that night.

In parting, I shook the hand of my dear co-worker, then threw my arms around him. "We have been through so much together over the past twenty-five years," I said, "and now we must part again. I will keep praying for you!"

"We'll meet again for sure in the glorious heavenly kingdom," he said.

As night neared we stopped at a village and asked a passerby where the inn was. The man looked at us in fear, then pointed to some ruins. Only charred beams and mud bricks remained where the inn had stood.

"The innkeeper refused to pay them the money they wanted, so they butchered him and burned his inn."

"Who did it?" I asked.

"Why, the Red bandits, of course. They say they're bringing in a new order and there won't be any rich people anymore. Everybody will share the wealth of the rich and have the same amount of land and money."

"Then why do they plunder and kill?"

"They say they have to break the spirit of the rebellious and pave the way for the new order. By the way," he continued, "they hate all American imperialists! You had better avoid them."

"Where are they now?"

"Hiding in that mountain. About five hundred of them." He indicated with his chin the direction we would have to go. "They plunder the trucks that try to get through."

"How can they stop the big trucks?"

"Roadblocks," was his laconic reply.

The following day we started out early, hoping to negotiate the dangerous curves of the highest mountain while we had daylight. We said nothing about what was uppermost in our minds, for there was only one way to go.

As I looked anxiously toward that mountain, the words of the Psalmist flashed into my mind and I quoted them aloud: "I will lift up mine eyes unto the hills, from whence cometh my help? My help cometh from the Lord."[3]

Moments later we came upon a scene of destruction: a burned truck, pieces of clothing, broken boxes. We passed in silence. A while later, the scene repeated itself.

The day had been clear and bright when we started out. But at noon, nearing a summit, an ominous dark cloud moved in and enveloped us. We could barely see the road ahead. We crept along in tense silence.

Suddenly a dark mass loomed ahead. I jammed on the brakes.

For a few moments we sat as if listening to the idle of the engine. My heart beat wildly. A barricade of rocks and branches blocked the road. Quietly, I opened the car door.

"Where are you going?" Ada whispered intensely.

"To clear a way through." I began to pull away branches and heave rocks.

"I'll help," said Elsie, petite as she was.

Together we worked with the strength that arises from an emergency. Having cleared a path, we drove through, almost in disbelief that we had not been attacked.

Farther on we came to another barricade. Again we worked feverishly to clear an opening, expecting to be set upon at any moment. Again, nothing happened as we cautiously drove through our opening and then sped on our way.

At last, descending the mountain, we came again into clear sunshine. As we drove into the town of Sha-ch'iao in the foothills, we met a large convoy of trucks lined up along the road. The soldiers stared as though we were ghosts. Then a babble of excitement started, and a crowd thronged around us.

"How did you get here?" asked an officer, looking in bafflement at our dusty Dodge.

"Over the mountain road," I answered. "There is no other way."

"You must have had a very powerful escort," he said, incredulously. "Where is it?"

I started to say we had no escort. Then I pulled out my Chinese Bible. "Our escort came from up there," I declared, pointing to heaven. "This Book tells about the great God, the Creator, who controls all things. He sent His cloud to cover us so we could come through safely." And then we seized the opportunity to share the gospel with our hearers.

When we arrived back in Kunming after an absence of almost two months we received notice from the American consul, advising us to leave China as soon as possible. Because of the increasing lawlessness and violence, the American School had to close. We decided to send Elsie and Irene with other missionaries on a plane to Hong Kong where they would board a freighter bound for the United States.

It was a tearful farewell. Both girls clung to us. "Please don't stay any longer than you have to," they begged.

Margaret, too, left to return to her home in England.

We had been asked by our missions board to see if we could stay and work under the Communists. We continued ministering as we could while rebels gained more and more control. Hostilities increased. Soon we could no longer go and preach in either city or village areas.

People with position or means were a special target for brutal attack. Atrocities increased. Wherever the Communists gained control all religious belief and practice were systematically destroyed.

A second warning came from the American consul: In Communist-controlled areas there was no protection for foreigners against arrest, detention, trial, and mob action; neither was there freedom to move about—or leave. All missionaries therefore were strongly advised to leave the country before the means of leaving was cut off.

We realized that if we stayed, our presence would also jeopardize our national co-workers and believers. Therefore, with aching hearts, we bid them farewell one November day in 1949.

This meant good-bye to mainland China.

------

[1] 1 Kings 18
[2] Psalm 112:7
[3] Psalm 121:1,2

The Lisu coming up to
the convention

Two Lisu boys, Methu-
selah and Abednego,
value their Bible picture
cards

Leonard Bolton ministering at the chapel (Notice the gospel posters.)

Gathering of Pentecostal missionaries in the Second Southwest China Conference of the Assemblies of God, Kunming, 1948

National workers at the conference: Pastor David Ho and Evangelist Jonah

Congregation of *Fu-yin T'ang* ("Happiness News Hall") in Kunming

Margaret, Elsie, Leonard, Irene, and Ada before the departure from China

Leonard Bolton examining some Lisu literature (John Ho is at the right.)

24
Other Fields

The sorrow at leaving China was tempered with the joy of being reunited with our children. We spent Christmas, 1949, in Springfield, Missouri, where all three were attending Central Bible Institute (CBI). Times together as a family were few but very précious.

We had consented to a request from the Missions Department to fill a need for ministry in Jamaica, in the British West Indies; so we made the necessary preparations and left in the spring of 1950.

Life on this beautiful tropical island was quite a contrast to life in the snow mountain areas of Wei-hsi and the metropolitan crowds of Kunming. Our rented bungalow near the town of Mandeville, up-country from the capital city of Kingston, had plenty of windows to catch the breezes. We circulated in ministry at such places as New Green, Hatfield, Ballards Valley, and Treasure Beach.

In 1951 our son, after graduating from CBI, ministered with us for six months. He helped me make pulpits and signs for our chapels. Then he, Ada, and I ministered together in many churches around the island. We especially enjoyed our visit to the far western point, Westmoreland, where we had been invited to preach in a rarely visited but thriving church of several hundred members, as well as at four branch churches. The kind, elderly, distinguished-looking leader, Pastor Lawson, was a grandson of slaves from East Africa. He was respected as a chief by his people.

The Jamaicans were friendly, relaxed, and unhurried. They spoke a charming Pidgin English. Their singing was spirited, as they rhythmically clapped on the offbeat. And they loved to testify. All of them seemed to be "born preachers." Services were informal and often lengthy. Sometimes the testimonies were amusingly unconventional.

One hot day in a brush arbor service dedicating a new chapel site, we were seated in a place of prominence on the improvised platform. Testimonies and speeches were many and long. After a couple of hours we were fighting drowsiness.

Just then a black Jamaican woman of ample proportions came ambling in and walked straight up to the front. After receiving a nod of consent from the leader, she proceeded to "give a word." She said, "While I was out there washing a pile of clothes the Spirit of the Lord came upon me and told me to come to the meeting." She went on, waxing more and more eloquent, ending by saying we were all one family in the Lord.

Then, finalizing her "message," she pointed to Robert and said, "This is my brother in the Lord." Turning to Ada, she said, "This is my mother in the Lord." She then turned to me and I expected her to say "my father in the Lord," but with a dramatic flourish of her hand and in all seriousness, she declared, "And this is my *husband* in the Lord!" And with that, she thanked the congregation and leader and ambled out again to resume her washing. Our drowsiness fled in the effort to keep a straight face, for the congregation saw nothing amusing or unusual about the incident.

That summer Elsie and Irene came to Jamaica for a couple of months. Together we conducted vacation Bible schools for all ages and held services in churches all over the island. So, in the midst of busy ministry, we had the joy of being together as a family again. All too soon the time came for the children to leave.

During our two years in Jamaica we also assisted two congregations in completing their chapel buildings. It was gratifying to see the churches grow in members and maturity.

The Lord's hand of protection was upon us in Jamaica as it had been in China: When a destructive hurricane ripped through the island, church buildings were damaged but, thank God, none of the believers suffered injury.

One hot day while I was taking a swim in the beautiful tropical water off the southern coast, some nearby fishermen shouted an excited warning for me to "Get back to the beach. Quick!" I did! They had seen the furtive shadow of a shark lurking nearby in the water. That attacker could have been as mean as any bandit in China.

Our furlough of 1952 was highlighted by two weddings. Our younger daughter, Irene, married William Riddle, a graduate of CBI. Our son, Robert, married Evelyn Burke, also a graduate of CBI and daughter of Rev. Fred Burke, an Assemblies of God missionary in South Africa. Both couples began pioneering new churches, the former in Massena, New York, and the latter in Somerville, New Jersey. Elsie went into evangelistic ministry.

A NEW AREA NOW CHALLENGED US: the city of Chittagong, East Pakistan. And we were jolted by a new travel adventure: being left in a foreign port by our ship as it sailed away with our baggage and passports. We had sailed into Bombay and been told our ship would be docked for several days. So we went to visit and uplift some discouraged missionaries at Poona, but we forgot to carry our passports. Imagine our dismay on arriving back at the dock to find the freighter gone! An unexpected schedule change caused it to sail earlier.

We reported our predicament to the shipping agent, who in turn reported us to the police. The police declared us to be aliens without passports going to East Pakistan, which they considered an unfriendly country. Until temporary permit papers could be acquired, we were put under house arrest at the YMCA.

Since the ship was to circle around the southern tip of India, we were permitted to leave Bombay and travel across India by train to Calcutta where we could board it once more. Huddling under newspapers trying to keep warm during those long, cold nights on the train, we wondered why this had happened. Later we understood. In Calcutta we were invited to preach in a Chinese church. One of the members gave us the address of a Chinese family in Chittagong, named Wang. Having someone to contact at our destination, which had no Pentecostal witness, meant a great deal to us.

Mr. Wang welcomed us at his tannery. He introduced us to some of his friends and helped us rent a house on Chandmari Road. At first our days were less than peaceful because of the constant blare of Indian music from a store across the street. But the Lord helped us adjust to the different environment and to endure the heat. He blessed our small beginning. The Sunday school grew and Mr. Wang later became the superintendent. In services we had a mixture of people: Chinese, Tamil-speaking Indians, and those of the Moslem faith. The love of the Lord brought them together.

One day we visited a young Anglo-Indian mother, Cynthia. She was grieving over the loss of her baby boy. "A priest told me that since my baby was not baptized, he is in limbo. He cannot go to heaven," she lamented, "and I will never see him again."

"Oh no!" said Ada, comforting her. "Your baby *is* in heaven."

"How do you know that?" Cynthia asked in surprise.

"Because I have two little baby boys in heaven myself," Ada told her. "The Lord Jesus invited the little children to come to Him. He said 'of such is the kingdom of heaven.'[1] He also said that to be saved we, too, must become like 'little children.'[2] If you trust in Christ, Cynthia, you can be saved, and you will see your baby boy again, in heaven."

Finding someone who had also known sorrow, Cynthia opened up to Ada and was led into a glorious experience of salvation.

After a year's ministry, about twenty people were attending services at the Chandmari Road mission and another twenty at Dhampora, a second preaching point in the city. Twenty others who had been saved had moved away from Chittagong.

The following year the Lord had another move in store for us: a transfer to Burma. He provided for the furtherance of the Chittagong church by sending two fine missionaries, Josephine Spina and Elsie Marialke, to take over the work. After a great deal of red tape to obtain entry visas, we were on our way.

RANGOON, IN 1956, HAD CHANGED CONSIDERABLY since I had first landed there thirty-two years earlier as a new missionary. Formerly an important port city in British Burma, it was now the capital of the Union of Burma. Unchanged, however, was the glittering magnificence of the famous 2,500-year-old Shwe Dagon pagoda with its rich overlay of gold. And unchanged was the spiritual darkness of the people in a city of Buddhist monasteries, temples, and shrines.

Church planting here meant rock-bottom pioneering. We began in rented quarters on Windermere Road, with just a few addresses of people to contact. Later the Lord gave us two co-workers: an Anglo-Burman, E. Vedu, and a Tamil-Indian lay preacher, Felix.

Within a few months eighteen were attending services at the Windermere Road mission and twenty at Kankto, a preaching point on the edge of town. By June, we had baptized sixteen converts.

We welcomed to Rangoon a new missionary family, the Glenn Staffords. Glenn had previously served in the American armed forces in Burma. Now he was back with his wife and little daughter in the service of the Lord.

After they were settled, we moved over five hundred miles up-country to Mogok, to minister where fellow missionaries, the Walter Erolas, had pioneered. Mogok, with a four-thousand-foot altitude, was near the world's most famous ruby and sapphire mines.

Here we felt closer to our former ministry in China. We were overjoyed to meet Lisu people and minister in their language. Within a year, at two preaching points—one in Mogok and one at an outlying place called Chappi—a total of seventy Lisu were attending services. They were pleased to know we had ministered among their fellow tribespeople in China.

We also ministered to some Chinese. Among them were two men who, with their families, had fled Communist China. Mr. Li had been a prosperous tailor in northern China. With his sewing machine strapped to his back, he and his little family had left everything to seek freedom. They traveled over a thousand miles across China before settling in Mogok. By now they had become pratically destitute. Mr. Li heard the message of salvation from an evangelist and yielded his life to the Lord. The second man, a barber, also accepted Christ in Mogok.

In these two cases, I could see the hand of the Lord at work. Mr. Li had heard the gospel in northern China but had turned a deaf ear until, displaced and brought low, he was ready to hear the message. The barber had never heard the gospel in China. The Lord brought him a long distance to a place where he came into contact with the message and he responded. Both families had been uprooted that they might receive salvation. As the poet observed, "God moves in a mysterious way His wonders to perform."

In 1956 I experienced the greatest highlight of my missionary career. Rev. Maynard Ketcham, Field Secretary for the Far East with the Assemblies of God in America, and his wife Gladys visited us in Mogok. He invited me to accompany him into northern Burma to attend the Silver Jubilee Convention planned by Lisu Christians. I was elated at the prospect of once again being in a Lisu convention. Gladys Ketcham stayed with Ada.

We flew to Putao and then traveled by jeep. Believers had hacked a road through the jungle and even constructed bridges—all with hand tools. Riding along, my mind went back twenty years to when I had taken my first trips into the remote eastern parts of upper Burma, over the mountains from the China side.

Then I had been the sole white man, trudging by foot, not knowing what lay ahead. Now, in the company of Maynard Ketcham, I rode knowing we were to meet with hundreds of believers as well as the Clifford Morrison family. The latter had been ministering with deep dedication in Burma since 1947.

What an experience awaited us! What I had seen on a smaller scale in China, I now saw in mammoth proportions. Lisu believers with their axes had felled numerous trees and cleared four acres of jungle land. They had hewn out poles, woven ropes of bamboo and fiber, platted mats of leaves, and erected a tabernacle large enough to accommodate over two thousand people! They had also built a three-room bungalow of bamboo and fiber matting for the foreign guests: Maynard Ketcham, Walter Erola, and me.

The Lisu came from as far away as two weeks' journey. They brought rice, corn, other foodstuffs, and their sleeping mats. The host churches brought chickens, fish, and cows to butcher for food. They had devised an ingenious method of serving meals to the crowd of two thousand people. Long tables, each a hundred and fifty feet long, were made of split bamboo. A trough along the center of each table carried a stream of water. Individual portions of food were dished onto bamboo leaves along each side of the table. As they ate, people could dip into the miniature stream in front of them for drinking and washing purposes. The large crowd could then eat together without disorder or delay.

On meeting the general superintendent of the Burman Assemblies of God, Rev. John Fish, I was interested to learn he was Lisu.

Then, greeting his wife, I discovered she was none other than Hsi Chen, a playmate of our children at Wei-hsi! She had been adopted by the Harvey Wagners while they were in Yunnan Province.

The Lord greatly blessed the two-week convention. Lisu leaders led the morning, afternoon, and evening services. They requested Rev. Maynard Ketcham to minister daily. The other missionaries and I took turns preaching. Many believers received the baptism in the Holy Spirit during the times of praise and prayer. A marvelous sense of God's presence pervaded the atmosphere.

We were thrilled to learn the Burman Assemblies of God now numbered seven thousand, of whom the majority were Lisu. For the first ten years the Pentecostal work in Burma had been carried on by Lisu evangelists. Then the Morrisons entered Burma to live and labor among them, laying a solid foundation as the revival spread among the Rawang, the Maru, the Kanong, and the Burmans.

The greatest thrill for me was the first day of the convention when I heard my name called excitedly by a group of Lisu who had just arrived. Their faces were beaming.

"How do you know my name?" I asked in surprise, shaking hands with them warmly.

"We remember when you came and preached in our villages many years ago on the other side of the China border," they explained. "You and Pastor Ho brought the message of salvation and we believed. The Communists tried to take away our faith. We managed to escape over the border. Here we are free to worship and to tell others of the Saviour."

"What of those who are still in China? Do you know if they have remained true to the Lord?" I asked.

"Oh yes!" they replied. "Not only have they remained true, but the number has grown. Thousands believe now. Many have suffered severely. But the Communists cannot stop God's Holy Spirit from working!"

I was elated by this news, but also humbled and deeply grateful to have had a small part. I was thankful that love's labor, in those long exploratory trips and circuit ministry among the tribes, had not been lost. God was continually bringing forth fruit in His kingdom.

Some months later in Mogok we received a shocking notice from the government. We would have to leave Burma immediately because of a technical error in our visa.

Uprooted again, and just when things seemed so promising! A Chinese church had been started at Kaukna with a Mr. Lu as its leader. In the six places we were holding meetings, attendance already totalled one hundred seventy.

Naturally we were loathe to leave. But once again we committed all to Him who is the Lord of the harvest and does all things well.

In the providence of God, the disruption allowed us a timely visit with our son Robert and his wife Evelyn in Taiwan, where they were serving as missionaries. Their little Sharon was the first of our grandchildren we had seen. Robert and Evelyn had lost their second baby due to an Rh-negative blood problem. Doctors had said it would be impossible for a third baby to survive. But God had given them the promise of another child. We found them believing the Lord despite medical evidence indicating the pregnancy would be unsuccessful.

Many people in the States, and Evelyn's family in South Africa, were praying. And Ada, ever the prayer warrior, took up this burden and prayed earnestly.

The result was a miracle. The baby was born perfectly normal, having no need for a blood change. They named her Marvel Joy.

"This is the name the Lord gave me for her before she was born," explained Evelyn. "The doctors would marvel and we would have joy!"

And I had joy, too, in dedicating her to the Lord.

As we ministered in Mandarin Chinese at a couple of churches in Taiwan, we felt that after our furlough we should serve our final term on this island and then retire.

OUR FURLOUGH WAS DELAYED FOR A YEAR, however, while we filled another need, this time to pastor a church in Kohala, Hawaii.

Our lives certainly did not lack variety. We drove through sugarcane fields and looked down over shaggy cliffs to the Pacific Ocean below.

As in Jamaica we could use English in ministering to the islanders.

Many people were out of work because of a strike and the needs were great. Among those to whom we ministered was a woman who had suffered with an ulcerated leg for nineteen years. She was marvelously healed! The Lord continued to bless the people.

Back in the States on furlough we got to see our other grand-children, the three daughters of Irene and Bill, now a police officer. We also met for the first time Elsie's husband, Domenick Ezzo, a pastor, and our first grandson, Randy. These family joys were doubly delightful after the many years and many miles of separation.

God gave us a fulfilling and enriching furlough. People responded to our messages. My heart burned with missionary texts of the apostle Paul: Romans 1:15—"As much as in me is, I am ready to preach the gospel"; Romans 1:14—"I am debtor both to the Greeks, and to the Barbarians"; and 1 Corinthians 16:9—"A great door and effectual is opened unto me." Our great desire was to see others receive a divine call and respond to this highest of all challenges— so demanding, yet so wondrously rewarding—the call of missions.

EARLY SUMMER OF 1960 saw us happily sailing by freighter to Taiwan. Robert, Evelyn, and our two little granddaughters excitedly welcomed us at the southern port of Kaohsiung. Joyful times together as a family merged with hard work: getting our goods through customs, setting up housekeeping in a rented Taiwanese house, being introduced to the churches Robert and his co-workers had been pioneering, adjusting to the high humidity and heat.

A large gospel tent we had brought was put to use right away for a Pentecostal conference in Taipei. Notable guest speakers were Rev. J. Philip Hogan, executive director of the Foreign Missions Department of the Assemblies of God; Rev. Frank Boyd, Bible teacher and writer; Rev. Paul Pipkin, missionary-evangelist; and Rev. Yumiyama, general superintendent of the Japan Assemblies of God. Quite an array of languages was heard: English, Japanese, Mandarin Chinese, and Taiwanese. The Holy Spirit unified our hearts as we praised the Lord.

We found the island of Taiwan a microcosm of mainland China's religion and culture. Never before had we seen such a concentration of idolatry, coupled with the many and varied traditions of the Taiwanese folk religion. The density of population, all bent on material survival, complicated the task of penetrating the masses with the gospel. But we did see God's Spirit at work, drawing out a people for His name.

Robert, Evelyn, and the children sailed for the States in November, planning to visit Evelyn's family in South Africa along the way. She had not been home for twelve years. Our hearts felt empty after they left. But much was to be done in the two cities of Kaohsiung and Fengshan. We also held a Saturday night gathering for some American servicemen and their families who were hungry for the Word of God.

I felt led, in my preaching, to emphasize the need for the baptism in the Holy Spirit, and several believers received this glorious promise of the Father. The Lord also miraculously healed a child of a serious chronic lung disease.

At the Chinese New Year in February 1961 I assisted the Taiwanese pastor, Robert Chou, in baptizing seven people in his Fengshan church. A highlight was the idol-burning ceremonies in the homes of two families. On both occasions the families took down their family idol and altar, ancestral tablet, incense sticks and pot, idolatrous papers, and the shelf on which all these had been placed. Everything was publicly burned as a testimony that a clean break had been made with their idolatrous past. They were instructed to put up gospel texts and pictures in place of the altar. What victories the Lord gave us!

We had heard of tribespeople in Taiwan's mountains. They were few in comparison to the vast throngs in the cities and towns of the plains; nevertheless, we wanted to visit them. The opportunity came when a friend, Pastor Timothy Chou, invited us to preach in a Paiwan tribal village in the foothills about forty miles to the east. My message in Mandarin Chinese was interpreted into the Paiwan dialect. Twenty people responded to the appeal for salvation. Their simplicity stirred some chords deep in my heart.

That night as we lay in our sleeping bags on the *tatami* (grass matting) floor of a Paiwan house, Ada said to me somewhat wistfully, "Doesn't this remind you a little of Lisu country?"

I had been thinking the same thing. But the similarity was only enough to be a reminder. My mind went back to those happy years and in my heart was still a great yearning.

---

[1]Mark 10:14
[2]Matthew 18:3

Two thousand people attended the Rawang Silver Jubilee Convention, 1958. Front row, left to right: Glenn Stafford; Walter Erola; Clifford, Lavada, and Geraldine Morrison

Rev. John Fish and his family. He was general superintendent of the Burman Assemblies of God for many years. His wife, Hsi-Chen, was adopted by the Harvey Wagners and grew up in Yunnan Province, China.

Silver Jubilee convention ferry!

Leonard Bolton talking with a Lisu friend

Along a hilly trail, a Lisu woman coming to the convention

Photos by Maynard Ketcham

Taiwanese believers seeing Ada Bolton off at the Kaohsiung Railway
Station

Leonard Bolton dedicating granddaughter Marvel Joy
to the Lord, 1958

Epilogue

Robert Bolton and his wife Evelyn arrived in sunny South Africa after a month's voyage on a freighter. There, in the southern hemisphere, they enjoyed the Christmas season in summertime weather. They had a family reunion at Spring Valley near Witbank, Transvaal, where Evelyn's father was principal of the African Bible Training Institute.

Ada's letters from Taiwan told of busy, happy ministry. Then word came that Leonard had been stricken with a severe heart attack soon after his sixty-first birthday. He was in the Adventist hospital in Taipei. A cable arrived later to say that he had passed into the presence of the Lord. Robert and Evelyn were stunned. They had left Leonard in a seemingly strong and healthy condition, especially in view of his having had to pass certain medical requirements before being given his new missions assignment in Taiwan. Upon receiving the news, Robert and Evelyn claimed a prayer of Solomon: "The Lord our God be with us, as he was with our fathers: let him not leave us, nor forsake us."[1] Although his father was gone, Robert and his wife found comfort in knowing the Lord would not forsake them or Ada; He wanted them to carry on His work.

It was hard for the children to be half a world away from their mother. They had never been more widely separated: Robert in South Africa, Elsie in Pennsylvania, and Irene in California.

Knowing the circumstances of living in Taiwan, Robert was doubly anxious for his mother. She now did what surely called for the greatest effort and resoluteness of her life. She went back to the house that spoke so much of her husband, a house difficult for a woman alone, with its cumbersome iron-grill sliding door across its storefront-like entrance. Without the support of family, old friends, or even beloved nationals (the Taiwanese believers were still new acquaintances), she quietly took care of family matters and continued to minister to the churches. The Lord did provide support during this crisis, however, through two American couples who attended the Saturday night Bible study.

When Robert and Evelyn returned after their furlough, they learned the details of Leonard's homegoing. An excruciating beehive carbuncle (as the Chinese called it because of its multiple heads) might have affected his heart. Driving through the milling crowds in the narrow lanes to and from church added its own strain.

On the way home after one particularly heavy Sunday, the crowd jostling in the market street that night made driving especially taxing. Leonard showed signs of stress. Early the next morning, February 10, the heart attack occurred. Ada managed to contact a Norweigian medical missionary an hour's distance away. Dr. Olaf Bjorgaas hastily arranged for a Chinese Air Force plane to fly Leonard north to Taipei; an ambulance then transported him to the hospital. Ada followed by train. Fellow missionaries in the Taipei area came to visit and pray with him.

Ada stayed in his hospital room night and day. They prayed together, interceding for a spiritual awakening in Taiwan and China. At times Leonard prayed softly in a language given him by the Holy Spirit. Heaven's light seemed to be on his face. He rallied, then worsened rapidly.

On the evening of February 18, 1961, Ada was sitting by Leonard's bedside. Suddenly he raised his head slightly and looked at her.

"Ada, the record is finished." Then speaking more slowly, he said, "I will meet you in the morning." With that he lay back.

Bending over him, she thought he was gone. But he opened his eyes again, and she saw the "glory light" in them as he spoke again, "I can see them coming—the Lisu."

Ada kissed him gently and his head fell back on the pillow. She knew he was gone. At that moment, spikenard perfumed the air, filling the room. She felt the Lord Jesus himself had come to receive her husband.

After thirty-seven years of faithful, fruitful service, Leonard Bolton was now in the presence of the Lord he loved and served.

As Ada stood in the rain and mud in the little foreign cemetery in Tamsui, supported by fellow missionaries, she was comforted by Leonard's last words. She could picture a heavenly parade of Lisu welcoming him as they had on earth, singing and shaking hands with the one who had brought them the message of life. What she could not know, then, was the prophetic quality of Leonard's last words.

Ada lived and ministered with her son and his wife for two years, completing her term. Her prayers, messages, and wise counsel affected the lives of both old and young. At age seventy she had a good send-off to the States for retirement.

Living in an apartment adjacent to the home of her daughter Irene in California, Ada brought blessing as grandma to three growing girls. She continued her ministry of prayer for hundreds of people, keeping a long list in her Bible.

Then romance blossomed again in a beautiful and appropriate marriage to a "retired" China-missionary widower, Rev. B. T. Bard. Both bride and bridegroom were nudging eighty! With him she traveled twice to minister in Germany, and once to speak at Bible institute graduation services in Hong Kong and Taiwan.

After more than five happy years together, Ada was widowed a second time when a heart attack took Rev. Bard to glory. Her sister Mary, long retired, came from Santa Barbara for the funeral. The two women, who had seen so much sorrow together, walked upright, arm in arm, still facing life with courage.

Mary died in her ninetieth year. Ada at eighty-five made the decision to spend her final years in Maranatha Village, a retirement home in Springfield, Missouri. In her uncomplaining and selfless manner, devoted to the Lord and the needs of others, continuing constant in prayer, she exemplified growing old gracefully. She died February 6, 1984. Like her sister, Ada was ninety years old.

THE PROPHETIC ASPECT OF LEONARD BOLTON'S last words has become evident in what God has been doing in recent years.

The Lisu *have* been coming—in great procession. And more than that, they have been in the forefront, leading a vast number of others to take up the torch of the gospel. This revival has continued to spread until in Burma today the Assemblies of God fellowship numbers over fifty thousand believers in five hundred established churches and outstations.

Having traced the Lisu Pentecostal Movement back as far as 1921, we saw how it began with the pioneer ministry of Alfred and Mary Lewer and her sister Ada Buchwalter (on the China side of the border). Later, Leonard Bolton, the Clifford Morrisons, and their daughter, Geraldine, brought the gospel and the fire of Pentecost to the Lisu on both sides of the border.

Leonard Bolton's ministry and the Burman Lisu work were twice linked: first, by Leonard's early exploratory trips with Pastor David Ho into upper Burma in the early thirties, contacting both Nung and Lisu tribespeople; and, second, by many Lisu of the Mekong and Salween River regions, brought to Christ under the ministry of Leonard and his co-workers and emigrating to Burma and becoming part of the great Burman church.

When these Lisu tribespeople from China settled in Burma, they had with them their Scriptures, songbooks, simple catechisms, and vibrant testimonies. Nung tribespeople associating with them saw their need of the gospel and asked for copies of the Lisu Scriptures, since their own dialect lacked a written script.

Then in 1931 an event occurred that marked the beginning of the Burman Assemblies of God.

Two Rawang tribesmen from Burma traveled over high mountain passes into the Salween Valley carrying packs of Burmese goat wool to trade for Chinese rock salt. They came to Shang Pa, where the Clifford Morrisons were living, and "happened" on a Pentecostal convention. There they heard for the first time of Jesus who could wash away their sins. One of the men, tears streaming down his face, waved his hand toward the west and exclaimed, "My people live beyond those mountains. . . . They have never heard the story you tell of the one True God, and know not the 'Way of Life'. . . . Won't you send someone to my people to tell them about Jesus?"

Because of the heavy demands, the Morrisons could not leave their work. But as soon as springtime melted the snows and opened the high mountain passes they sent two Lisu preachers. After only three months' ministry, thirty-seven Lisu and Rawang families had believed and put away their spirit shelves to serve the Living God. Other Lisu workers were sent later.

In 1941 when at last the Morrisons were able to visit Burma, more than five hundred believers gathered for worship in their first service.

"Great . . . was our joy and happiness," wrote Lavada Morrison,

> when . . . the power of God swept the whole building. People all over the church were shouting the praises of God and speaking in other tongues. . . . During our two weeks of meetings with them, above three hundred were baptized in water. . . . Also at this time the Burma churches were set in order. . . . Young prospective workers from the Burma side, for the first time, were assigned to the work under the supervision of older workers."[2]

For some time this revival continued under only the leadership of Lisu Bible students and evangelists who would travel among the newly developing churches and then return to the China side for more training themselves.

After the war, in 1947, the Morrisons entered Burma with their daughter, Geraldine, for missionary ministry. They labored among the people in extremely rugged conditions, living in houses constructed with wooden poles, thatched-straw roofing, and walls of mats woven with bamboo strips. The Lisu, who had built the houses for the Morrisons, planted vegetable gardens for them as well. They provided cows for milk, and goats, chickens, and pigs for meat. Because of the pressing need for Bible training of the new believers, the Morrisons conducted short-term schools in various places for as many as two hundred students. Following indigenous principles they laid a solid foundation for the tribal church in northern Burma.

IN 1956 THE LISU SILVER JUBILEE WAS HELD. This was followed by the Rawang Silver Anniversary, with the general superintendent, John Fish, in charge. Missionaries participated in both conventions.

A long-needed and planned-for resident Bible school to train tribal preachers was built at Myitkyina in 1964 by missionary Ray Trask, a newcomer to Burma, and his colleagues. A tribal preacher, Rev.

Walter Po Ang, who had graduated from the Assemblies of God Bible Institute of Malaya in Malaysia, became director of the school.

In central Burma, God was blessing at Mogok under the ministry of the Erolas. One church grew to a fellowship of five hundred people.

Meanwhile, down in Rangoon, God's Spirit had also been at work. From its humble beginning with the Boltons in 1956, the work developed further under the ministry of Glenn Stafford. During Stafford's time there, the Lord was preparing a very promising national leader.

Myo Chit had a rich Christian heritage. His great-great grandfather was one of six Burmese who accepted Christ under the ministry of the first, long-term Protestant missionary to Burma, Adoniram Judson, known as the apostle to Burma. At first Myo Chit was very antagonistic to the Pentecostal mission in Rangoon, calling it "that crazy church." Well educated, having studied in England, he was at that time employed by the American embassy in Rangoon. Then God baptized him in the Holy Spirit. Filled with joy and set aflame, he then associated closely with Glenn Stafford and the church. In January 1966, the Lord called him into full-time ministry. He assisted at the Rangoon church for three months until events suddenly thrust him into full leadership of the church.

IN MARCH OF THAT YEAR THE BLOW FELL. A government edict ordered all foreign missionaries to leave Burma within a month. Rev. Maynard Ketcham, Field Secretary for the Far East representing the American Assemblies of God Division of Foreign Missions, was sent to "wind things up" in the transfer of authority, responsibility, and all mission property and equipment to the national church leaders.

> It was an emotion-packed hour: it was the end of a mission era. I went with a commemorative plaque in my briefcase and a burning message on my lips. Making a manful effort to hold back the tears, I presented my plaque to Rev. John Fish, the Lisu general superintendent of the Assemblies of God in Burma, with these words: "Into your hands we give the torch. Hold it high! . . ."

Pastor Fish's reply is indelibly imprinted on my memory. "Pastor Ketcham, we are going to miss you, your missionaries, your material and spiritual benefits—but you are not going to take the Holy Spirit out of Burma, are you?"[3]

It was a touching scene; both the veteran missionary-executive and the new Lisu leader knew they depended on the Holy Spirit. And both knew the Holy Spirit could be neither taken away from, nor shut out of, any country.

One-and-a-half years passed. On September 30, 1967, Rev. Ketcham managed to visit Rangoon again on a twelve-hour visa. National leaders descended on the city from up-country. Together with other believers they held a great, rousing rally in what had become an overcrowded Rangoon Revival Center. It was a joyous, almost hilarious occasion.

And there was the Rev. John Fish with his broad grin and twinkly eyes! "How about it, Pastor Ketcham—when your missionaries left we had 180 churches, 12,000 believers, and 25 students in the tribal Bible school. Now we have 300 churches in a fellowship of 25,000 believers, and 75 students in the Bible school. See what the Holy Spirit can do!"[4]

What surpassing joy to learn that despite the descent of what Maynard Ketcham called the "teakwood curtain" the Holy Spirit had not been expelled from Burma!

In the Rangoon church Myo Chit had felt dismayed at suddenly finding himself in full charge. An old church building had just been purchased with mission backing, with plans to renovate it. The phasing out of the American mission left Pastor Chit with a heavy debt. The change in the government's attitude toward missionaries caused uncertainty. Attendance dropped to fifteen and lower. But under the Holy Spirit's power he forged ahead. People were healed in answer to prayer and many were converted.

Then the Lord spoke to an elderly woman who had attended just a few services. She gave Pastor Chit a check that completely canceled the debt on the church. A family, who did not personally know him, felt led to donate land that was their family inheritance. This site became a center for short-term training of hundreds of young people from all over Burma, many of whom had been saved in youth camps held in various locations.

The increased need for formal training of ministers prompted the opening of a Bible college. Twenty students immediately enrolled. Present at the inception of the new school (Evangel Bible College) was Rev. Wesley Hurst, Field Director for Eurasia, following Rev. Ketcham's retirement. A great rally was held during the short time his visa permitted him to be in the country. The people begged him to preach on and on, so hungry were they to hear God's Word.

IN 1980, REV. J. PHILIP HOGAN, EXECUTIVE DIRECTOR, Division of Foreign Missions, American Assemblies of God, obtained a seventy-two-hour visa to visit Rangoon. He was accompanied by Dr. Peter Kuzmic, a professor at the Biblical Theological Institute of the Assemblies of God in Yugoslavia. The Burman Assemblies of God leaders took full advantage of this short visit. Delegates and leaders thronged the Rangoon church to hear the esteemed visitors, who alternated ministering. Preaching was not by individual sermons; rather, it was by hours in round-the-clock sessions!

"What a joy it is," Rev. Hogan said, "to minister to people who come with a notebook and pencil and wait expectantly for every word you say, as if you were a prophet!"

At one point Rev. Hogan stopped preaching to inquire who in the congregation had come the farthest. After some consultation in the audience, three young men stood up. "How far have you come?" Rev. Hogan asked.

"We have walked fifteen days," they replied.

Thinking he had misunderstood the interpreter, Rev. Hogan said, "You mean fifteen miles?"

They protested in unison. "No, Pastor Hogan, we mean fifteen days!" The interpreter told their story. Coming from the northern part of Burma they had walked for fifteen days through jungle territory and over some of the world's steepest terrain. At night they slept beside the trail. When they came to the last village before the airstrip where they were to board the plane for Rangoon, they bathed in a river and changed into the clean clothes they had carefully carried.

This is what had fooled Rev. Hogan. "Here they stood," he marveled, "in fresh-pressed clothes that looked better than mine, since I had been living out of a suitcase in the tropics for three weeks!"[5]

These young men stood as a remarkable testimony to the effectiveness of God's Word and the sovereign power of His Spirit in one of the world's unlikeliest fields.

THE YEAR 1981 FOR THE BURMAN ASSEMBLIES OF GOD brought a celebration surpassing all others in magnitude—their Golden Jubilee. Since no American could go inland and visit the week-long convention, January 29 to February 6, a taped message of congratulations was sent by Rev. Hogan, representing the American Assemblies of God.

Almost sixty thousand people, representing many different tribes, came from all over upper Burma, as well as from the Mogok and Rangoon areas. Services were held in Jubilee Village, a town built especially for the occasion. The government of Burma had allotted a square mile of territory in jungle country to the church for this purpose. Prodigious labor went into its development.

The celebration opened with a mile-long procession. Various tribespeople marched in groups, arrayed in their distinctive colorful regalia. Rev. Myo Chit, now general secretary of the Burman Assemblies of God and superintendent of the Rangoon District, cut a ribbon, formally opening the convention. Festivities during the week included songfests, special music, and preaching by the leaders. Twenty pastors were ordained to the ministry. Huge throngs of people added to the excitement. Inspired by the presence of the Holy Spirit, God's people celebrated by rejoicing and praising the Lord Jesus.

A vital feature of the Golden Jubilee was the prayer garden called Gethsemane. Here, people fasted and prayed around-the-clock.

As He had the Israelites of old in the wilderness, the Lord protected His people in the jungle area. Reported Pastor Chit, "Although thousands of people were gathered together in one place, there was no sickness, theft, fire, or serious accidents."[6] Truly, this alone was a mighty miracle!

A plaque was presented to a government official, expressing appreciation to the government for the permanent gift of one hundred fifty acres of the original square mile. This site, called Jubilee Village, has developed into a settlement. Following the convention, five hundred families settled there, cultivating rice and planting orange and grapefruit orchards as a source of income.

The country around Jubilee Village near Putao and going eastward is totally Christianized. The majority of people among those little-heard-of tribes—the Maru, Kanong, Rawang, and Lisu—are Spirit-filled believers. They reside in completely Christian villages where, according to Maynard Ketcham, "the sign of the cross is the 'open sesame' to the social register. Willful sinners are banished—house and belongings—to the neighboring jungle until they repent, confess, and make restoration."[7] Such living is in contrast to secular society elsewhere.

"Today," writes Pastor Chit, "you can walk for days from Putao toward the Chinese border, and every village you pass through is an Assemblies of God village. Thousands have turned to the Lord Jesus. We call it 'God's country'!"[8]

ANY GREAT MOVE OF GOD HAS ITS ANTECEDENTS. The great spiritual awakening among the Lisu and neighboring tribespeople is no exception. The greatest secret of all has been *intercessory prayer.*

Seventy years ago, the CIM pioneer missionary J. O. Fraser, the apostle to the Lisu, was a man of much prayer. His burden extended beyond the reaches of his own mission, and his Lisu script became the vehicle of the message. Lavada Morrison's tears and prayers had an immeasurable bearing on the success of their work. Ada Bolton, too, was a prayer warrior who knew how to "touch the Throne of Grace." Jean Wagner, Ruth Ho, and others, together with untold multitudes in England and the United States, formed a barrage of prayer. The gospel seed was sown in tears and fervent intercession that brought it to fruition.

Another secret has been *sacrifice.* The Lewers, the Boltons, and the Morrisons forsook their homes and endured incredible hardships, wearisome travel, sickness, and even bereavement. Among the Boltons' relatives, nine graves in China and one in Taiwan bear mute testimony. David Ho and his son John were faithful unto death.

Missionaries also *identified* themselves with the Lisu tribespeople. They learned their language, customs, and culture; ate their food; and shared their problems—they loved them. This brought a response of love that spread to others.

Then there was *mobility.* The missionaries went to the people. In upper Burma, the Morrisons moved from place to place as opportunities arose for church planting and training of workers. They went to areas where they could most effectively reach the people, living in houses built for them by grateful tribespeople.

Finally, their Spirit-anointed preaching was coupled with *constant training of workers.* A solid foundation was laid according to indigenous church principles. Thus, when the missionaries had to leave both China and Burma, the tribal work went on and the Lord caused it to flourish.

WHAT OF THE CHINA SIDE OF THE BORDER? Despite persecution and the evacuation of many Christians, news comes through that Pentecostal believers among the Lisu now number twenty thousand—double the figure in 1956 at the time of the Lisu Silver Jubilee in Burma.

Some servants of God, like the heroes recorded in Hebrews 11, did not receive deliverance (v. 35). Word filtered through that Pastor David Ho was seized by Communist authorities and forced into hard labor, carrying heavy rock salt on his back. He was later imprisoned in Li-Chiang where he was left to die of starvation. His son John had previously been shot by soldiers while conducting a gospel service.

Out of such sufferings has emerged a church—an ongoing, triumphant Lisu church—looking with hope for a bright tomorrow.

Built right into the Chinese language is an expression of hope for the future. The word for "tomorrow" is *ming-t'ien,* meaning "bright day." Believers in Christ know this as more than just wishful thinking.

Imprisoned for years by the Burmese authorities in the last century, Adoniram Judson never gave up. As he translated the Scriptures into the Burmese language, he envisioned a great church in Burma. This hope is reflected in his immortal words: "The future is as bright as the promises of God!"

Leonard Bolton's dying words also pointed to a bright day. He looked beyond, to "the morning." And full of hope, he foresaw multitudes of Lisu coming—because, it should be added, he, along with others, responded to a call of God, a China call.

---

[1] 1 Kings 8:57

[2] Lavada Morrison, personal letter to Maynard Ketcham, circa 1947, pp. 3,4, archives, Division of Foreign Missions, Assemblies of God Headquarters, Springfield, Missouri.

[3] Interview with Maynard Ketcham, Springfield, Missouri, June 1982.

[4] Ibid.

[5] Philip Hogan, "Open the Word for the World," *Advance,* December 1980, p. 6.

[6] "Burma Assemblies of God Celebrates 50th Anniversary," *Pentecostal Evangel,* June 5, 1981, p. 10.

[7] Ketcham, Ibid.

[8] "Pentecost in Burma," *Pentecostal Evangel,* November 29, 1981, p. 15.

January 1961, over three thousand at the Burman Assemblies of God conference

The Golden Jubilee of the Burma Assemblies of God, 1981
Part of the choir, leading the mile-long procession in the opening ceremony

Golden Jubilee Scenes:
People leaving the main auditorium
Below, part of the crowd in the main auditorium

Rawang and Lisu choir members in their tribal costumes

Authors Robert (son of Leonard and Ada) and Evelyn Bolton, missionaries to Taiwan